Jennifer ~

Have Joy!

Karen + Lily

A Feminine MANIFESTA

LILY HILLS
KAREN HUDSON

A Feminine Manifesta
By Elizabeth "Lily" Hills and Karen Hudson

GODDESS TO GODDESS

Goddess to Goddess Presents
Post Office Box 4886
Carmel, CA 93921-4886, U.S.A.
www.GoddesstoGoddess.com

Unattributed quotations are by
Elizabeth Hills and Karen Hudson

Edition ISBNs
Hardback 978-0-615-35433-0

Library of Congress Control Number – 2009912803

Design and layout by Scott Hudson – Hudson Design Company
Printed in the United States of America

Books are available at quantity discounts for non-profit groups.
For more information please contact:
Goddess to Goddess Presents, P.O. Box 4886, Carmel CA 93921-4886
www.GoddesstoGoddess.com

This book is printed on partially recycled post consumer acid free paper.

To our wise, courageous and dedicated foremothers – and all the women who participated in the women's movements that afforded us the privileges, choices and freedoms we enjoy today.

Rest assured, we will pay it forward.

Acknowledgements

We would like to thank, from the bottom to the top of our hearts:

Scott Hudson - for your endless patience as we worked on this book, unfaltering belief in our project and in us. For your sweet loving support in every area imaginable, your sense of humor which was, at many times, a life line and for the fact that you worked well beyond the call of duty to allow for the creation of this book. We both adore you.

Katherine and Hugh Hudson - the bright lights in our lives, for your patience as we wrote the book, for believing in it all along, and for making us laugh throughout the process (especially at ourselves!) You are wise, kind and extraordinary souls and we are so grateful for the tremendous gift of you!

Joseph Krackeler - Thank you, Dad, for your support and continual faith in us and our project and especially for giving us a model of sharing abundance with those you love and believe in. It's such a blessing to know that you have my back in every way.

Margaret Jennings Krackeler - for showing both of us maternal love at an early age, guiding us to understand what it means to truly love and respect yourself and for always understanding the inherent strength, wisdom and value of women. Your angel spirit continues to guide us every day.

Barbara and Ned Hills - for your love, sense of humor and support as we made the transition from teenage girls to the women we are today. It is a blessing to share this incredible life journey with you, learning and growing from and with one another.

Our sisters Katie Marron, Alison Walecka, Catherine Breen and Jennifer Schaffer for your continued love and support throughout the book writing process and beyond.

Jane Waxman our wonderful editor for your wise counsel and keen editing eye throughout the book. Your prowess is hugely appreciated sister, and we feel fortunate to know you.

Nina Solomita, for your much appreciated editing talent during the final stages of this birthing process.

Joy Colangelo and Kimb Massey - for your early encouragement and guidance as we took this book from conception to completion.

Kenneth Appel for so elegantly modeling the balance of the masculine and feminine and for your incredible wisdom and support over the years.

Sandra Wilder Schnitzer, Jackie Priestley, Kristen DeKam, Helen Nazar Bishop and Dorothy Divack for being our most cherished wing girls and cheerleaders throughout life.

To all the women in our lives, too numerous to recount, who have modeled in so many extraordinary ways the transformational power of the feminine.

We love you all!

CONTENTS

Preface

The Birth of A Feminine Manifesta

We met on the first day of school in the fall of 1978, two nervous freshmen at St. Francis High School in Mountain View, California: Lily with her giant brown eyes and a mouth chock-full of silver braces, and Karen with her fiery red hair and Catholic uniform skirt hemmed just beneath the knees. We've been the very best of friends ever since.

For over thirty years, we've seen each other through thick and thin. New love, dramatic breakups, and marriage. Career success and financial duress. Health kicks and compulsive eating disorders. Births of children and heart-wrenching deaths of friends and parents. Fortunately, there have been more bouts of outrageous joy, adventure, and fun than hardship. Karen has been married to her college sweetheart for twenty-two years and is the mother of a teenage daughter and a pre-teen son. Lily is single and living life at its fullest in excited anticipation of meeting her true love. Although neither of us would say her life is perfect (whose is?), we *can* both say that as we enter our forty-fifth year, we are the happiest we have ever been and our lives continue to unfold in ways that surprise and delight us.

We're passionate about the work we do in supporting women to develop better relationships with themselves, and we're having more fun than ever since becoming five-days-a-week business partners. Of course it doesn't hurt to be soulmate friends—think Lucy and Ethel—who've been making each other laugh till we snort on a daily basis since we were thirteen. We're loving *almost* everything about growing older (yeah, the loss of skin elasticity we could do without). We're in the best shape of our lives and have never been healthier, stronger or more at peace. And most importantly, our relationships with our loved ones are flourishing.

This book was born out of the happiness we're experiencing that we want to share with other women. The original idea was hatched as we walked along Crissy Field by the Golden Gate Bridge about seven years ago. We were talking about how our own happiness seemed directly related to our ability to be kind and respectful to... ourselves. Women could be much less stressed-out, we agreed, if we weren't constantly picking at our own perceived flaws and inadequacies. It's like we've got an aggressive inner jockey—always riding ourselves with the whip instead of offering ourselves a carrot. We recognized the irony in this behavior, given that it's exactly our self-critical ways—and the accompanying crankiness, insecurity and frustration—that drive us all to act in ways we're not proud of.

It occurred to us that day that we women have unknowingly disempowered ourselves as a gender in large part because of our lack of self-appreciation. We were speaking from personal experience, each carrying her own torrid history of being self-critical. It had taken both of us many years of therapy, voracious reading, countless seminars, endless chick-chats and some darn good coaching before we finally saw the idiocy of our old self-demeaning ways and made a pact to lighten up on ourselves.

Slaying—or at least badly maiming—the dragon of self-denigration, we discovered, brought out our more patient and loving sides, which made us like ourselves more and ultimately allowed us to create more connected relationships. When it finally sank in, the lesson seemed so simple and obvious: being loving to ourselves was a much smarter choice than the alternative, not only for our own good, but for the good of our families, friends, and any random stranger that crossed our paths.

Warming to our topic, we walked and talked for hours on the trail along the San Francisco Bay. "We should write a book and share this holy grail o' wisdom with as many women as possible!" we declared. Every woman, we vowed, should know the truth—when a woman is kinder to herself, not only does she feel happier, but it also brings out the best of who she is. Our enthusiasm crescendoed as we envisioned the message of empowerment we wanted to share with our sisters all over the world. Naïve as first graders, we figured we could crank a book out in no time. Really, how hard could it be?

Well, as anyone who's ever written a book knows, it's *really* hard and takes endless hours of hardcore focus. We became impatient with the process but simultaneously so excited about all the information we accumulated that we simply couldn't wait any longer to share what we knew.

So instead of finishing the book, we decided to offer seminars for women. How hard could it be? Well, the seminars were fantastically inspiring and empowering—if we do say so ourselves—and the ladies who attended left high as kites, armed with all sorts of stress reduction techniques and self-appreciation tools, to say nothing of a much stronger sense of their own inherent value. But getting women to take time out of their busy schedules and commit to a weekend of self-reflection was like pulling teeth with extra long roots. Additionally, many of the seminar attendees reported that once they returned to their daily routines, they'd fall back into old habits of self-criticism.

So *then* we thought, "Let's make it easy for them: let's bring the mountain to Mohammed and do a weekly radio show. That way we can connect with even more women continuously in their homes and cars. How hard could it be?" *The Goddess to Goddess Empower Hour—Inspirational Information for Women and the Divine Dudes Who Love Them* was birthed from this place. We *loved* doing the radio show; it was a complete blast and it got rave reviews in our tiny Monterey Bay community, but it turns out breaking into the national radio market would require years of knocking on doors traditionally closed to female empowerment programming. Once again, we simply didn't want to wait to get our message out to the masses.

So here we are, having come full circle and back to the book you now hold in your hands. Whoa, what a wild ride!

When we first started writing again, we were bursting with even more great information and we wanted to share *all* of it, every juicy morsel of wisdom we'd gleaned from our own experience and the "life experts" we'd interviewed each week on *The Goddess to Goddess Empower Hour*. The first version of the book—twenty eight verbose chapters, each dedicated to a specific practice—elicited the following admonition from a friend: "Honey, women like me are gonna be devouring this thing between diaper changes at home and filing briefs at the office. Think pamphlet, not epic saga."

She was right, of course. After more months, revisions, and cups of coffee than we care to admit, we whittled *A Feminine Manifesta* down to three simple steps, the three most powerful practices we know of for creating a phenomenal life based on a healthier relationship with yourself. Each of the practices is related to your feminine side—and each is connected to self-love, which we believe to be the most important facet of happiness. Take what you like from what we offer, and leave the rest behind, but be sure to give each one a try.

Writing *A Feminine Manifesta* has been one of the most profound and challenging experiences of our lives. We wrote it to support *other* women in living in more joy—but, because we've immersed ourselves in the practices in this book for all these years, we've ended up taking our own lives to much higher levels. Are we the authors practicing everything we preach? Absolutely. Are we doing it perfectly? Of course not! Are we much stronger, kinder, wiser, joyous and peaceful than ever before? Without a doubt. This is why we can recommend these practices to you with complete and utter confidence.

Thank you for investing in this book, and in yourself. We feel privileged to be a part of your journey.

- Lily Hills and Karen Hudson

The Plight of Women in the 21st Century

We women are hard on ourselves:

I look fat in these pants • I was way too hard on my daughter today •
I did such a poor job on my presentation • I'm always late • I hate the
way my hair looks • I'm so forgetful • I can't get my act together •
I'm not pretty • I can be such an idiot • I shouldn't have said that •
I wish I was thinner • I'm not good enough • I'm always losing it with
my kids • I'm not a good cook • I can be such a bitch to my husband
• I have no self control • I'm not qualified for that job • My breasts
are too small • I'm not a very good friend • I look fat in these pants
• I was way too hard on my daughter today • I did such a poor job on
my presentation • I'm always late • I hate the way my hair looks •
I'm so forgetful • I can't get my act together • I'm not pretty • I can
be such an idiot • I shouldn't have said that • I wish I was thinner
• I'm not good enough • I'm always losing it with my kids • I'm not
a good cook • I can be such a bitch to my husband • I have no self
control • I'm not qualified for that job • My breasts are too small •
I'm not a very good friend • I look fat in these pants • I was way too
hard on my daughter today • I did such a poor job on my presentation
• I'm always late • I hate the way my hair looks • I'm so forgetful • I
can't get my act together • I'm not pretty • I can be such an idiot • I
shouldn't have said that • I wish I was thinner • I'm not good enough
• I'm always losing it with my kids • I'm not a good cook • I can be
such a bitch to my husband • I have no self control • I'm not qualified

We tend to pay attention to what we don't like about ourselves instead of what we like.

What I wouldn't do to have a body like hers, mine's so flabby • *Her house is so beautifully and elegantly decorated, mine looks so outdated and cluttered* • *She's so accomplished and confident, I feel like a loser compared to her* • *I'll never be as pretty as she is* • *I feel like an idiot compared to her* • *Her skin is so much more beautiful than mine* • *She seems to have it so together, why can't I be more like her* • *Her hair is so much thicker than mine* • *I wish my husband would look at me like that* • *She is so much smarter than I am* • *Her life is so much more fun and interesting than mine* • *She doesn't have any of the crows feet that I do* • *I wish I could be like her* • *Her kids seems so well adjusted* • *Why does she get to have it all* • *She's a nicer person than I am* • *I wish I could be you* • *I wish I had her easy going life* • *How does she stay so organized?* • *I'm never seen her in the same outfit twice* • *What I wouldn't do to have a body like hers, mine's so flabby* • *Her house is so beautifully and elegantly decorated, mine looks so outdated and cluttered* • *She's so accomplished and confident, I feel like a loser compared to her* • *I'll never be as pretty as she is* • *I feel like an idiot compared to her* • *Her skin is so much more beautiful than mine* • *She seems to have it so together, why can't I be more like her* • *Her hair is so much thicker than mine* • *I wish my husband would look at me like that* • *She is so much smarter than I am* • *Her life is so much more fun and interesting than mine* • *She doesn't have any of the crows feet that I do*

We make ourselves feel inadequate by comparing ourselves to other women.

5

I don't want to hurt her feelings, so I have to do it • I can't work out, the kids need me • He comes first • We've got to spend the holiday with my parents, they'd be so hurt • It's okay, I'll watch your kids so you can go out • I don't have time for dinner with my girlfriends, my husband needs my help with the kids at bedtime • I can't say no to her, she'd be devastated • I'll work late so you can go home • I don't want to risk our friendship • I've got to do it or it will never get done • I'm so tired but, sure, I'll go • I'm not hungry, but I'll eat with the family •

I don't have time for my friends, my family has to come first • I don't know wh

We often put the needs and well-being of others before our own.

they'd be so hurt • It's okay, I'll watch your kids so you can go out •

I don't have time for dinner with my girlfriends, my husband needs my help with the kids at bedtime • I can't say no to her, she'd be devastated • I'll work late so you can go home • I don't want to risk our friendship • I've got to do it or it will never get done • I'm so tired but, sure, I'll go • I'm not hungry, but I'll eat with the family • I don't have time for my friends, my family has to come first • I don't know where I'll find the time, but you can count on me • I'll work late so you can go home • I don't want to risk our friendship • I've got to do it or it will never get done • I'm so tired but, sure, I'll go • I'm not hungry, but I'll eat with

I only worked out once this week • My house is such a mess • I hardly got anything checked off my to-do list today • I didn't spend enough time with the kids this weekend • I should be feeding my family healthier food • I should have sent a birthday card • I should have helped with the schools fundraiser • I should have finished that report • What was I doing all day? • I've got to get organized • The garden hasn't been weeded in months • I should be better about recycling • I can't believe I forgot her birthday • I need to volunteer more • I should have brought her a hostess gift • I should have gone to college • I should have been more successful by now • I should workout more • I should have thought ahead • I shouldn't have eaten that • I should have planned better • I only worked out once this week • My house is such a mess • I hardly got anything checked off my to-do list today • I didn't spend enough time with the kids this weekend • I should be feeding my family healthier food • I should have sent a birthday card • I should have helped with the schools fundraiser • I should have finished that report • What was I doing all day? • I've got to get organized • The garden hasn't been weeded in months • I should be better about recycling • I can't believe I forgot her birthday • I need to volunteer more • I should have brought her a hostess gift • I should have gone to college • I should have been more successful by now • I should workout more • I should have thought ahead • I shouldn't have

We judge ourselves for not doing enough.

7

These self-defeating thoughts and behaviors make us far less confident, peaceful, and happy than we could be. In fact, they make us feel downright insecure, impatient, cranky, depressed and unhappy. Of course, when we judge ourselves so unkindly that we make our own lives miserable, we're likely judging everyone else harshly and at times making their lives miserable, too. Our internal self-condemnation may even manifest in external forms of self-abuse like compulsions and addictions to food, drugs, cigarettes, work, control, cleaning, or shopping. Compulsions and addictions compound our troubles not just because they tend to be unhealthy physically, but also because they give us more reason to berate ourselves.

But that's not the worst of it. The truth is that our less evolved "shadow" personas—the bitchy, gossipy, overly competitive, impatient, judgmental, and compulsive sides that emerge when we're hard on ourselves—contribute to our tarnished reputation as the weaker sex.

Ouch! That hurts to admit. But now the cat's out of the bag and running around on the table where it can no longer be ignored. As big fans of women and passionate women's empowerment activists, we're loathe to acknowledge that we women have played a role, albeit an unintentional one, in our own sullied reps. But let's face it: when we've dished about a co-worker behind her back or yelled obnoxiously at our husband within earshot of the neighbors, we've embodied negative female stereotypes and inadvertently given weight to the general consensus that women are the weaker sex.

Most of us women already know we play a role in how we're perceived. But what we *don't* know is that our less-than-desirable behaviors are always driven by a conflicted relationship... with ourselves. Women are showing up in the world at a fraction of our incredible potential specifically because we lack this awareness.

The intention of *A Feminine Manifesta* is to address this plight head-on. Only when women can recognize the direct correlation between our self-denigrating thought patterns and our negative behaviors can we escape this destructive cycle and liberate *the very best of who we are*. And at this time in the course of humanity, the world needs the very best that *all* of us can offer.

> *Women are often as hard on each other*
> *as we are on ourselves.*

Interestingly, the belief that women are members of the less empowered sex doesn't just exist among men. While it's true that most women love, respect and count on our intimate circle of female friends, many women don't respect, like or trust other women. Instead of appreciating the unique gift that each of us offers, women are in the habit of measuring our physical attractiveness, our financial position, our career success, our marriage and even our children's achievements in relation to those of other women. And we often resort to gossip, unfair assessments and hostility when we feel intimidated and threatened by another woman, rather than striving for excellence as individuals independent of what anyone else is doing or achieving.

Honestly, we've all got a story or two about being hurt, betrayed or even sabotaged by another woman. Some of us have been stabbed in the back at work by a female colleague we trusted. Others have had our husbands or boyfriends "stolen" by another woman. Some have experienced extreme jealousy and competition from even our very best girlfriends.

In her book *Tripping the Prom Queen: The Truth About Women and Rivalry,* Susan Barash examines the complicated and dark side of female bonding. Barash's study of female subjects of all ages, races, and backgrounds illuminates the often un-recounted rivalry and envy at the heart of many women's relationships. "Despite all the efforts of the women's movement to change this troubling pattern," Barash laments, "we're still willing to cut each other's throats over what we value most—jobs, men and social approval. We tend to ignore men when it comes to competing, focusing our rivalry almost entirely upon each other." Barash describes women's friendships as both empowering and disabling, "a source of rock-solid strength as well as a mire of treachery, deceit, and misunderstanding." Data from her studies reveal:

- More than ninety percent of women of varied social strata claim that envy toward other women colors their lives.
- More than sixty-five percent of women say they are jealous of their best friend or sister.
- Eighty percent of women report having encountered jealousy from other females since grade school.

- Ninety percent of women in diverse jobs report that competition in the workplace exists primarily between women, rather than between women and men.
- Forty percent of women describe themselves as victims of another woman's theft of a husband, lover, boyfriend, or job.[1]

Clearly, our competitive relationships with each other, both personally and professionally, are bringing us misery. So why do women continue along this destructive path?

For starters, most of us weren't exposed to an early female role model whose self-esteem was intact and whose level of self-awareness was particularly advanced. You were the exception if you had an imperturbable June Cleaver-like mother—or grandmother—who sat you down early on and explained that when you speak disparagingly of another, judge someone without compassion, or compare yourself to anyone else, you generate a myriad of negative consequences not only to you as an individual but also to women as a whole.

What's most tragic in this scenario is that because women haven't *consistently* brought forth the most powerful part of who we are—our wise, confident, compassionate, understanding, patient, self-respecting and courageous selves—we've been confined to more limited roles in our society. The glass ceiling is still an obvious reality, with women earning 78.7 cents to every dollar earned by men in comparable positions.[2] Although women make up forty-eight percent of the work force, we hold fewer than eighteen percent of the top management jobs.[3] And although we represent more than half the world's population, women constitute only sixteen percent of national parliaments and are heads of government in only seven nations out of one hundred ninety.[4] We have inadvertently fueled the misogyny that has kept us from equality, diluting our influence in political and social arenas where our participation would be of immeasurable benefit.

While it's fair and accurate to say that women have been, and continue to be, undervalued, underestimated and held back by societal pressures, media, ignorance, and institutionalized misogyny, it will do us no good to point the finger without recognizing our own role in the problem: that our society doesn't value us more in large part because we don't value *ourselves* more. As Virginia Wolfe said, "Women are simultaneously victims of themselves as well as victims of men."

> *Our culture mirrors our relationships with ourselves.*

It's not about picking on the ladies here—*A Masculine Manifesto* is coming on the heels of this book. Rather, it's about taking responsibility. We women *must* own our part in what we've co-created before we can build the awareness that not only are we *not* the weaker sex, but we are an extremely powerful one. Only when we recognize our own complicity in sabotaging the reputation of women will we be able to shake up the status quo that prevents us from manifesting our full potential in the world.

Women are Truly Divine

If we women could see ourselves clearly, without the thick film of our own self-judgment clouding our vision, our self-esteem would rise dramatically because we are *extraordinary* creatures. We are naturally caring beings: the very first to show up when a friend is in crisis, volunteer for fundraisers at the pre-school, stay up with a sick child, remind our friends of how wonderful they are, reach out to those less fortunate and put our own needs aside in order to concentrate our efforts on those we love. We are givers in the strongest sense of the word, innately heart-centric and immensely sensitive to the suffering of others. We want those we love to be happy and prosperous and we want the world to be a more peaceful place for our children and future generations.

When we women are ready to cast off the heavy yoke of self-judgment and celebrate ourselves openly for all that makes us extraordinary, we can more readily access and activate the powerful, self-confident, persuasive, caring, patient, collaborative and diplomatic qualities possessed by all great leaders. And then, without a doubt, more of us will be naturally inclined to seek or accept positions of leadership.

Why Women Make Great Leaders

It's obvious that men and women are very different creatures, but what makes women uniquely suited for positions of leadership? In large part it is our priorities. In her book

Marketing to Women, gender-based marketing specialist Martha Barletta discusses a cross-cultural study revealing the stark distinction between men's and women's values. The men in the study, reports Barletta, *overwhelmingly* wished to be seen as bold, competitive, capable, dominant, assertive, admired, critical, and self-controlled. Women *overwhelmingly* chose a very different set of descriptors: warm, loving, impulsive, generous, sympathetic, and affectionate.[5] Another recent workplace study reveals that while men value pay and benefits, achievement, success, status and authority above all other workplace interests, women rank friendship and relationships, recognition, respect, communication and collaboration higher than any of the preceding attributes.[6]

It's clear from these and many other studies that the primary goal of men is to continually gain ground in terms of "ranking." Whereas men are typically hierarchical in nature, women tend towards more egalitarian paradigms. Internationally renowned social scientist Dr. Riane Eisler contrasts the male style of communication and interaction—the "dominator model"—with the female "partnership model."[7] Simply put, according to Eisler's research, men generally care more about being top dog and women care more about the well-being of the pack.

> *The number one aspiration of women is to make the world a better place.*[8]

Generally speaking, women are hard wired to recognize that our level of evolution as a species is more accurately reflected by the degree of peace in the global community than by our technological, scientific, economic or military prowess. It is in the very nature of women to cooperate and compromise, to forge "win/win" scenarios—which is what makes women excellent candidates for positions of power and authority. Former President Clinton's press secretary, Dee Dee Myers, is in strong agreement with this assertion. In her book *Why Women Should Rule the World*, she argues that while women rulers may make their fair share of mistakes, they bring to the job an innate tendency towards cooperation coupled with a desire for peace that can significantly reduce violence in its many forms. Myers backs up her postulation by pointing out that women would make every imaginable sacrifice and consider every possible compromise to avoid sending their sons and daughters to war.[9] So true, so true! Clearly, there's much to be said for having world leaders whose priorities are less about saving face or achieving domination and more about building peace.

Your Role

Even those who do not seek positions of leadership have a significant part to play in the betterment of the planet. There is no such thing as a small role when it comes to creating a more peaceful world, and you are just as critical to the process as a senator, ambassador or a CEO. You can make a massive contribution simply through your personal evolution as an individual.

When women as a gender embark upon the journey of learning to value ourselves on a more intimate level, then collectively we will be a force to be reckoned with. We will cease competing with one another and instead come together to make our top priority, making the world a better place, a reality. But before we can move in this direction as a unified front and at our full potential, every one of us ladies will need to enlist the aid of one of the most powerful, healing and unifying forces on the planet: the feminine.

"Enlightenment involves cultivating all the feminine and all the masculine elements of ourselves, regardless of whether we are biologically male or female."
-Buddha

CHAPTER ONE

Introduction to the Feminine

Each of us, man and woman alike, has both a masculine and feminine side. Generally speaking, your masculine side is mind-oriented, aggressive, active, strong, productive and dominating. Conversely, your feminine side is heart-centered, nurturing, calm, gentle, patient and empathetic. The masculine and feminine aspects of your persona possess distinct—and equally important—characteristics.

When you need to deal with the details of life and accomplish your goals efficiently, it's crucial that you engage your masculine, the part of you that ticks things off the To Do list, that gets in there and gets the job done. Masculine energy is sexy; it is capable, achievement-oriented and virile.

In fact, you can spend all day in masculine mode, getting an endorphin rush from finishing the report at work, cleaning the house from top to bottom and making four dozen brownies for the PTA bake sale. But life will ultimately feel like a series of endless lists, tasks, responsibilities and worries, with very little peace and harmony, if your masculine is not tempered by your feminine.

The feminine is what keeps you connected to *you*. It's the compassionate voice that hushes the critic in your head whenever it insinuates that you are inadequate. It's the sidekick who reminds you of your inherent value, independent of how you look or what you achieve. The feminine is that tall, cool glass of water you pour yourself on a scorching hot summer's day.

The feminine doesn't only show up in your relationship with yourself; it also shows up in your relationships with other people. The mama bear who hugs your child when he comes home from school crying because someone called him a "spaz." That's your feminine in action. The ally who reminds your girlfriend to lighten up when she's being hard on herself. The nurturer who arranges some much needed downtime for your overworked and stressed husband, and the patient audience who listens to your aging mother complain about her sciatica yet again. That's right, it's your feminine, the part of you that's gentle and compassionate, not only with people you know and love, but even with the well meaning grocery cashier who's once again put your strawberries in the bottom of the bag.

The ancient concept of yin and yang that permeates Chinese science and philosophy illustrates perfectly the interconnectedness of the masculine and the feminine. Yin and yang are complementary opposites that, when balanced, provide that feeling of wholeness and centeredness where happiness is the norm. Yin and yang do not merely exist in static duality, however. The two are actually dependent on each other for their own dynamic existence and transformation—much as neither root nor fruit could flourish for very long without the other.

Clearly, both the masculine and the feminine are powerful influences for good. Drawing attention to the *distinction* between the two will allow you to determine which of these gender essences characterizes your own *modus operandi*, so that you can integrate each more actively to create balance in your daily life. In balancing your masculine and feminine, you will not have to give up anything you value. You will be at your most peaceful and productive simultaneously, able to *flow* through your days rather than *power* through them. Simply put, when there is equilibrium between the masculine and the feminine, life gets much, much easier.

The Feminine: The Antidote to "Overdoing"

Do you feel victimized by your busy-ness, unable to stop *doing* for fear you'll fall behind? Is it hard to feel like you've done enough or *are* enough? Does the thought of stopping in the middle of the day to sit and just *be* seem like an impossibility? If you haven't smelled anything but your dirty laundry basket, car fumes and the carpet in your cubicle since the '90's, you're likely a productivity junkie. In other words, you're short on the feminine, the missing ingredient that reduces stress and allows you to enjoy your days while your masculine simultaneously handles responsibilities.

Chances are, you've unwittingly minimized the feminine's presence in your life because you're too busy being busy. The devil-may-care childhood days of just *being* are phased out in adulthood, replaced with an all-time high of *doing* by sheer virtue of the fact that we're inundated with responsibilities, from picking up the dry cleaning to writing a dissertation. No wonder so many of us are reaching for chocolate bars, a martini or OxyContin. We long for a reprieve from the pressures of multi-tasking.

We women don't have many balanced role models to follow, since almost all of us have fallen prey to the dominant masculine energy of our culture. We're like innocent lemmings, following each other down a path of collective dissatisfaction, scratching our lemming heads and wondering why we aren't happier.

Disturbingly, this trend of hyper-productivity and busyness that diminishes the feminine appears to be intensifying. Multi-tasking is a way of life for most women and we excel at it. But just because a culture exhibits a behavior *en masse* doesn't mean it's normal. The behavior is simply what people have adapted to, given their social and economic priorities and cultural influences.

Mary, a freelance project manager and mother of two school-aged children, shares her insights about her hyper-productivity with fellow participants at our stress reduction workshop:

I was so committed to being productive I made the toughest drill sergeant look lackadaisical. There was no end to how clean my house could be, how much time I could devote to my job or how much I could sacrifice for my children and husband. I could have worked twenty-four hours a day and still not had the feeling I was ahead of the game.

I'd focus on what I hadn't accomplished rather than all the tasks I'd powered through. Thoughts like, "Aargh! My house is a mess and I still have grocery shopping to do and an expense report to finish before tomorrow—I'm never going to be able to fit it all in!" Often I'd tense up to the point where I'd feel like I couldn't breathe.

Even when my body was crying out for rest, it never occurred to me that I could literally STOP right in the middle of the day if I wanted to, just sit down for a little while and rejuvenate.

Alas, Mary's story is not atypical. Many of us women have embodied the masculine in order to "make it in a man's world." Our over-functioning behavior is stimulated in part by the corporate culture that rewards the hardest workers, those who put their careers before anything—including their mental and physical health. In addition, we're responding to the social expectation that if women are going to do "men's jobs," we have to do them with the same tenacity, aggressiveness and competitive spirit as men, rather than rely on our own innate feminine sensibilities to rewrite the script.

The question we women *should* be asking ourselves is: do we really want to perpetuate the behaviors that characterize "a man's world?" The more women engage in a hyper-busy, productivity-centric lifestyle, the more we contribute to a culture that's out of whack, and the less connected we become from the balanced life for which we so yearn.

Take a moment to clearly define your most heart-felt values as an individual. Now write them down (yes, that means *slowing down*—right now). Chances are your list of priorities looks something like this: peace of mind, free time to spend with family and friends, health, contribution, joy, fun on a daily basis, and so on. Now consider your daily existence: are you spending your hours in a way that fully supports your highest aspirations as a human being? Or have you tethered yourself to a lifestyle that's running you ragged, chasing a goal that, when it comes right down to it, isn't even all that important to you?

Making the Shift - The Power of the "Slow"

Slowing down in virtually everything you do—driving, eating, speaking, making decisions and even physical activity—

is *essential* to inviting the feminine into your daily life. In theory, it sounds simple, yes? But the idea of deliberately slowing down might be so antithetical to your normal way of being that right now you're thinking, "Yeah, right! Fine for somebody else. But I simply can't afford to slow down."

The truth is, when you take the time to consciously slow down, you'll end up being *more* productive. Instead of making choices from a place of rush or even panic, you can accurately assess your options and then choose wisely from a centered position. It's like sharpening your axe before felling a tree.

Here's Mary again, sharing her experience of slowing down:

When my best friend gently suggested I might benefit from taking a break in the late afternoon (typically my crankiest time), I resisted with all my might. Seriously? A walk in Mother Nature, snuggling up with a good book, or simply sitting still at 4:00 on a Monday?! "She's single," I thought. "She doesn't get that you don't have the luxury of stopping to relax in the middle of the day when you're a working mother."

My response to my friend's suggestion was downright angry—and that's when I finally realized something must be off-kilter in my thinking. Where, I asked myself, did I get the idea that I couldn't possibly stop and rest, at any time of the day, when I was feeling overwhelmed? What was it that made me feel like I couldn't get off the treadmill, even if I wanted to?

When I started paying closer attention, I had to acknowledge that I actually felt anxious when I was still. I didn't know how to quiet my manic mind, so, quite frankly, productivity was my escape from it.

Once I started giving myself permission to take breaks, life was far less stressful. I actually became significantly more productive because I was able to manage my time more effectively. I could make better choices, which prevented me from spinning my wheels and over-committing. Eventually I let go of a lot of my unreasonable expectations of myself and learned to trust what felt right for me and my family. I can't tell you how much lighter and more fulfilled I feel now.

> The feminine voice reminds you that **what you get done** is not nearly as important as **who you're being** and how you're **feeling** as you're getting it done.

Going into "slow mode" will help you—sometimes instantly—feel more relaxed. It will enable you to become more aware of what's happening around you and will give you access to a full range of subtle emotions and responses—including, of course, joy. And it will allow you to be more flexible and less reactive in your daily life. Rather than hurriedly shooing the kids out the door for school, you'll take that extra moment to hear about how Maddy Torres got stung by a yellow jacket at recess yesterday. Rather than devouring a 4:00 pm chocolate bar to quell your anxiety about the mounting pile of deadlines on your desk, you'll take a five-minute walk in the sunshine and return to manage each task more efficiently, without having to correct mistakes you made hurrying. Instead of rushing through dinner, you'll savor the flavors and textures of your food and draw out your meal like a great conversation.

If there's any question remaining in your mind about the benefits of *slow*, think of how many details you notice and appreciate when you're walking, compared to when you're anxiously speeding along in your car. Or imagine the effect of a slow, sensual kiss as opposed to a perfunctory peck.

The not-so-secret secret of slowing down is that when it's incorporated into your daily existence rather than reserved for special occasions, it can do more to improve the quality of your life than almost any other factor. The rush you used to get rushing around doesn't come close to the high you'll feel when you're luxuriantly flowing through your days. When you take your time in everything you do, you'll get a sensation similar to the one you experience on vacation, where you glide from one activity to the next, rather than racing around like a chicken with your head *and* a wing cut off.

The Feminine—It's Not Just for Women Anymore

Famed psychologist Dr. Carl Jung, the founder of analytical psychology, argued that we're not whole, well-rounded, balanced human beings unless we integrate the masculine and feminine sides of our personalities. Both men and women should be *thrilled* and *grateful* that they have a feminine and masculine side; this duality is part of what makes each of us an interesting, multi-dimensional human being.

So it's interesting to note that when you tell a *man* he has a feminine side, more often than not he'll act like you've slapped him in the face rather than patted him on the back. Men may love the feminine in us women, and they almost always want more of it from us, but rarely do they want to acknowledge the feminine in themselves. This is in part because men tend to confuse the feminine with weakness, or with the weaker behaviors we gals sometimes exhibit (i.e. cattiness, bitchiness, emotional combustibility). The macho model of masculinity is still very much alive, and it prevents men from embracing a very powerful and attractive part of who they are.

> Men bring out the best in themselves when they integrate their feminine side with their masculine.

"The newly evolving man," according to author and gender relations expert David Deida, "is not a scared bully, posturing like some King Kong in charge of the universe. Nor is he a new-age wimp, all spineless, smiley, and starry-eyed. He has embraced both his inner masculine and feminine, and he no longer holds onto either of them. He doesn't need to be right all the time, nor does he need to always be safe, cooperative, and sharing, like an androgynous Mr. Nice Guy. He simply lives from his deepest core, fearlessly giving his gifts, feeling into the fleeting moment into the openness of existence, totally committed to magnifying love."[10]

For the most part, men are not yet tapping into the fact that the *real* sexy—for both men and women—comes with a dynamic integration between the masculine and feminine. Sure, we want our guy to be able to fix the broken washing machine and pay the bills on time, but when he exhibits his gentle, tender, compassionate, cooperative and sensitive nature, it's a *huge* turn on. Knowing when the aggressive and direct masculine is appropriate, and when the caring and open feminine is fitting, creates a win-win situation not only in the boardroom, but also in the bedroom. This integration takes practice, a little trial and error if you will, given that most of us have gotten ourselves firmly entrenched in our own static ratio of masculine/feminine over time.

As we women learn to dance skillfully between feminine and masculine energy, we can bring a new vitality to our relationships and show men through our example how intoxicating the feminine can be. When we cultivate a gentler tone in our communications, stay calm in the face of a challenging situation or let go of activities and commitments that are creating extra stress, our men will take note and will not only be delighted with the shift towards the feminine, but will likely be inspired to follow suit. *Our* balanced embodiment of the feminine and masculine creates a safe space for men to express the softer side of themselves, serving to help bring *them* into balance as well.

> *Men will feel safe to accept their own feminine sides when they know they can count on and trust ours.*

Lynn, a pre-natal nurse who's been married for ten years, describes how bringing more of the feminine into her life has benefited her marriage:

After suffering a big loss in the stock market right after finishing a major kitchen remodel, Marty and I could no longer make our house payments. I was mortified to have to turn to my parents for money, and furious at Marty for allowing us to get into so much debt. We had some pretty nasty knock-down-drag-outs over who was more responsible for the situation. He blamed it on my spending too much on extras like French doors and granite countertops and I blamed him for his bad choices in the market.

I spent many a sleepless night contemplating how

I was going to approach mom and dad for money. For days on end I berated Marty. After one particularly ugly argument, I retreated to our bedroom and had a good, hard cry—which eventually led to an epiphany. By being so hard on him, I realized, I was only bringing us, the "team," down. I was crippling our ability to weather the storm of our financial crisis by sinking our ship under the weight of my judgments. I also recognized that until I took responsibility for my own role in what Marty and I had co-created, I wouldn't be able to forgive him for his part.

I went out to the family room where my poor guy was recovering from our blow-out and apologized for my angry behavior. I explained that I was so mad at myself, I'd been taking out my frustration on him. I promised then and there that I was going to handle things differently. And I'm proud to say that I did. Every time a money conversation was creating stress, I stopped for a moment, breathed deeply and carefully considered my responses, consciously defaulting to a feminine approach whenever the heat was turned up. Eventually Marty came to trust "the new me" and through my example, he learned to use his feminine side in his communications with me. Our new style of interaction eliminated much of the drama we used to experience and allowed us to deepen our relationship as we focused on solutions to our predicament.

Cultivating the Feminine

When you approach your partner with a gentle request rather than a demanding stance, isn't he more receptive? When you guide your children with patience, aren't they more cooperative? When you're supportive with your peers and co-workers, isn't it easier to create a collaborative team atmosphere? Of course! The feminine is powerful medicine, and when you offer your feminine qualities to everyone with whom you come into contact, you're gonna be one popular gal. It will feel good just to be in your presence.

But remember if you're reserving your kinder, gentler, more appreciative and compassionate side only for *other* people, if you're not lavishing it on yourself as well, then you're essentially serving the main course to your loved ones every night and feeding yourself the leftovers. If you really want to have full access to the benefits that the feminine brings, it's imperative that you learn to offer it to yourself too. Otherwise, your frantic, overworked, critical side will surge unchecked and spill over to those you care about the most. And then *everyone* will be unhappy.

A Feminine Model

So, now you've made a commitment (a gentle commitment) to make the shift toward a softer, slower, more compassionate way of being. But where to begin? For starters, it's helpful to have a model of the feminine to give you something to emulate.

One of the most familiar and relatable models we have of the feminine is embodied in the love a mother feels for her child. Mother-love, in its purest form, encompasses the very best of the feminine: gentleness, compassion, tenderness, appreciation and encouragement. This love is unconditional and infinite. So, in order to direct the feminine at yourself, you will want to create a mental model of an internal loving mother.

She will be different for everyone, of course. You might imagine your feminine as your own mother, or perhaps a grandmother or a very loving friend. Or your feminine might be represented by a religious mother figure such as Mary, Tara, or Quan Yin. She might even take the shape of an angelic being or a Mother Earth entity. Create your mental model of the feminine based upon the most compassionate image of a mother you can visualize, the one that makes you feel the safest and the most loved.

How might your "internalized mother" directly benefit you in everyday life? Well, instead of berating yourself when you forget to put postage on your mortgage payment, give audience to the gentle mother's voice that suggests, *That's okay, honey, we all make mistakes. That's what makes us human.* Instead of chastising yourself for having gained a few pounds, tune into the compassionate reminder, *You're beautiful at any weight— and besides, who you are on the inside is far more important than what you look like.* Instead of cursing yourself when you back your car into a fire hydrant, hearken to the wise maternal prompt, *Oh my, there's a message here; you must really need to slow down.* There's always a loving voice inside your head to counteract your inner critic and guide you with compassionate wisdom. All you have to do is slow down to hear her.

If you *really* want to tune into your inner feminine ally, don't just slow down, but sit down, breathe deeply, and allow yourself to enter into the restful place where the feminine resides. Remind yourself that a panicky or rushed pace is probably what got you in trouble in the first place. Then take that sweet mother love and shine it on yourself!

> *The more you direct feminine compassion*
> *towards yourself, the happier you will be.*
> *This practice is the ultimate*
> *form of self-love.*

"You, yourself, as much as anybody in the entire universe, deserve your love and affection"
-Buddha

Chapter Two

Self-Love

Why We Don't Love Ourselves Enough and Why We Should

If you could do one thing to positively impact the planet each day, and you knew that one thing would be really good for *you*, too, would you do it? Would you commit to that step? Yes? Good! Because the truth is, you only *need* to commit to one powerful, life-changing act to make a difference in the world. You simply need to be more loving, gentle, nurturing, compassionate and understanding with the person with whom you'll be spending the rest of your life: you. Your ability to be the best person you can possibly be in the greater world is *directly* related to how much you appreciate, respect and honor yourself.

Easier said than done, of course. We women already know we should lighten up on ourselves, but we're either not sure how to go about doing it or we're having difficulty breaking out of a self-defeating pattern. Some of us don't even realize how often we berate ourselves. Like sufferers of the dull, chronic ache of a bunion, we've become accustomed to the nagging of the inner critic who tells us we look fat in those pants, or we should have done a better job on that presentation.

The conflicted relationships we women have with ourselves don't just bring *us* down; they negatively impact everyone with whom we come into contact. The harder you are on yourself, the harder you are on others. When you judge yourself for how you look, you're more likely to be critical of other people's physical imperfections. When you're impatient with yourself for your inability to focus on one thing and get it done, you're more likely to be impatient with your kids for doing the same thing. When you're unforgiving with yourself, you're more likely to hold a grudge against your partner. More on *that* topic—judgments towards *others*—is coming soon, in Chapter IV.

> *The harder you are on yourself,*
> *the harder your life will be.*

Most of us are living our lives at a small fraction of our joy potential simply because we weren't taught the fundamentals of self-love. If, like many of us, you were raised by a mother who perfected the art of self-sacrifice rather than self-love, or who had such a difficult time seeing her own value that she was abusive not only towards herself but to you as well, you assimilated a model that prepared you to spend a lot of time and energy doubting yourself and your abilities. The good news is that you have the power to fashion for yourself a new model— one that's based on nourishing and loving yourself. Self-love is the most essential factor in creating and sustaining a fulfilling life because it impacts every single aspect of your existence, whether it's the vibrancy of your health, the status of your career, the robustness of your bank account, or the connectedness of your relationships with significant others, children, friends and even a higher power.

What's the first thought that pops into your head when you imagine practicing self-love? Do you envision yourself embarking on an endless circuit of manicures, pedicures and facials? Having lunch with "the girls" and crowing about your latest purchase, vacation or success? Neglecting your children because you're so preoccupied with your own wants and desires? Vanity, indulgence, and excessive self-absorption are *not* characteristics of self-love. In fact, they point to the exact opposite of self-love—low self-esteem, which is often masked by overconfidence, selfishness or even a superiority complex. We all know someone who attempts to buoy her fragile ego by dominating the conversation with unsolicited updates on her love life or her son's report card. By contrast, people who have a healthy self-appreciation are more likely to be curious about other folks than to bring excess attention to themselves. Authentic self-love does not preclude caring deeply about others. In fact, self-love adds *enormously* to one's ability to do so!

> *Self-love is a generous, wise and healing undertaking, not just for yourself, but for anyone with whom you come into contact.*

When a woman loves herself, she possesses a deep sense of inner contentment. She enjoys her own company. She feels neither superior nor inferior to anyone else, recognizing that humans are all equals, regardless of our life circumstances. She censors herself when she is tempted to judge, recognizing that judging is harmful to her own well-being as well as to that of others. Her self-respect is reflected in her choices: she surrounds herself with loving, supportive, healthy people; she balances work, play and leisure time; and she faithfully cares for her body.

She understands her limitless capacity to manifest her deepest heart's desires, so she's never envious of what other people possess. In fact, she's totally psyched for others when good things come their way. She takes action to change the circumstances of her life that cause her consternation and surrenders to events that are out of her control. When she makes a mistake, she sees it as a learning experience and is compassionate with herself. As a result of all these self-loving behaviors, she is so happy and fulfilled that she gives to others out of sheer gratitude rather than obligation.

> *The degree to which you honor and love yourself dictates the extent to which you offer unconditional love to others.*

Mastering the art of self-love turns us into more loving friends, wives, sisters, mothers, teachers and leaders. The world is in desperate need of more individuals who truly love themselves and bring their most loving selves to their personal and professional lives as well as to leadership roles that influence the well-being of the planet.

So take a moment to contemplate a simple but profound question: Do you have a loving relationship with yourself? What's your gut instinct? If you're not totally clear, answering these questions will give you a little extra insight:

- Is it easier for you to take care of others than it is to take care of yourself?

- Do you berate yourself when you make a mistake?

- Are you more likely to focus on your inadequacies than your strengths?

- Do you often feel like whatever you're doing isn't good enough?

- Do you frequently compare yourself to other women?

- Do you engage in compulsive behaviors like overeating, overdrinking, overspending and overworking?

- Do you often neglect your physical well-being?

If you answered "yes" to most of these questions—and most of us women will—it's a sign that there's room for you to improve your self-love quotient. But before you can tackle your self-defeating behaviors, you need to have an understanding of where they originated. Consider carefully what lies in the way of treating yourself as well as you treat your loved ones—can you name it? Why might you sabotage your desire to be happy by indulging in behaviors that bring you down?

Some social science experts have identified the influence of one's family of origin to be the dominant factor in the development of our relationships with ourselves. Others have argued that cultural influences play the most significant role in defining our self-value. Still others have suggested that how we feel about ourselves is simply a matter of genetics. The nature/nurture debate is an old one, and most contemporary experts agree that all three factors play a role in the development of self-esteem. Ultimately, determining the origins of your current relationship with yourself isn't as important as defining how you want to improve it. But it's worth taking a quick gander at your past to see how it's influenced your present.

Your Family Dynamic

If you're consistently able to make healthy choices for yourself, you were likely raised in a home where you were affirmed, appreciated and made a priority. Your parents were most likely raised in a loving, nurturing environment, too, which is what gave them the tools to help you develop a healthy sense of self. Conversely, if you find that you're repeatedly engaging in unhealthy behaviors such as addictions, self-criticisms, and relationships that are detrimental to your well being, it's a clear sign that you're operating from that part of you that was impacted by negative and painful early childhood experiences and hasn't fully healed—your "wounded child." Your parents probably suffered from a lack of respect and kindness from their own parents, and thus weren't given the resources to impart these qualities to you.

> *On an unconscious level, you treat yourself as an adult the way you were treated as a child.*

The psyche of a child is incredibly delicate and impressionable. When a parent bombards a child with *you're a bad girl, you're driving me insane,* or *you're so selfish—and after all I've done for you,* a child not only believes in that *moment* that she is flawed, but she also develops an impression of a flawed self that she may continue to carry throughout her life. (The possible exception to this generalization is when a parent apologizes, corrects the unkind statement and asks for forgiveness.) Children consider their parents to be the ultimate authorities. If a child perceives that her own parents see her as inadequate, she's likely to grow up believing it to be true. Many parents don't understand that unkind words and harsh tones, as well as physical violence, leave behind emotional shrapnel that children carry embedded in their psyches.

Damage to one's self-esteem can also take place in more subtle ways—as when, in the journey towards finding her authentic self, a child is intentionally or unintentionally sabotaged by parents or caretakers who have their own idea of who she should be. Psychiatrist and family systems theorist Dr. Murray Bowen attributes our self-image to intra-familial relationships. He asserts that while we're searching for our best selves—learning who we are and what we're capable of accomplishing—our personal journey is constantly interrupted by parents who scold, shame, or withhold love when our behaviors or choices don't match their expectations. Deep hurt and confusion results if, at this stage in our development, we don't receive the acceptance we desire at the deepest part of our being.

An individual whose sense of self has been injured can come from a very loving and well-meaning family. And even the most centered, loving and conscious parents "lose it" at times and lash out at their children. Most parents are doing the very best they can, and yet pretty much all of us have a wounded child. The point here is not to judge our mothers and fathers for the way they parented, but rather to understand with objectivity the role your childhood experiences played in contributing to your self-esteem—or lack thereof—so you can begin to repair the part of you that was diminished in childhood. Here are a few more questions to help you recognize the dynamics of your early years that may have impacted your self-esteem:

- Did you feel safe sharing your fears, worries and problems with your parents?

- Did you sense that your feelings were important to them?

- Did you feel like your parents loved you for who you were, or did you have to adapt to who they wanted you to be?

- Did you sense that your parents were preoccupied or present?

- Did you feel that you were their main priority?

- Did your parents seem generally happy or unhappy?

- Were you generally treated with respect by your parents?

- Did they express their love for you verbally and physically?

- Did they express their anger or disappointment in healthy and mature ways?

- Did they use physical punishment or verbal abuse to get you to obey them?

- Did they make you feel inadequate in any way?

- Were both of your parents addiction-free during your childhood?

- Was there sexual abuse in your family?

- What unhappy, shaming or traumatic childhood events stand out for you?

Core Beliefs

During childhood we establish what are commonly known as "core beliefs." These beliefs that you hold to be true create a frame of reference to help you make sense of your life experiences and of life in general. You can establish a deeply held core belief—"I am an idiot"—based upon a single event, like being told you were an idiot by your angry father when, at age three, you decorated the living room wall with crayon. Or a core belief—"Asians are shy"—can be based on a series of experiences, such as walking to school with a shy Asian classmate over a period of years. From these examples we can see that core beliefs are not always accurate, but rather are based on limited experience, subjective impressions and even cultural biases. Core beliefs can be both negative and positive.

The negative core beliefs we hold about ourselves are often a result of particular early interactions with our parents or caregivers. If your parents were neglectful of your emotional or physical needs, your core belief that you're "unlovable" or "not good enough" may cause you to neglect your body or constantly put others' needs before your own. If your parents were abusive, you likely developed a core belief that you are "bad" and deserving of abuse. You may subsequently abuse yourself by developing addictive behaviors, choosing unhealthy relationships, or indulging in chronic self-abasement. People who come from abusive backgrounds often mistreat not only themselves, but can also mistreat those around them. When you believe, consciously or subconsciously, that you are bad, not good enough or unlovable, you will sabotage your own happiness by attracting people and experiences that confirm this belief.

Your negative core beliefs, if not revealed and healed, can sabotage your life because they influence every thought you have and therefore every choice you make. By offering *yourself* the love you might not have received as a child, you can actually heal the psychological wounds that are impairing your perception of yourself and impacting your choices. By practicing the art of self-love, you can actually *rewire* that part of you that doesn't feel deserving or worthy on some level. But before we show you how, let's take a look at yet another influence that has strongly impacted your relationship with yourself: the culture in which you live.

Our Culture Impacts the Way You See Yourself

Cultural influences—behaviors, beliefs, values, traditions, biases and symbols—are passed along by communication and imitation from each generation to the next. The familiar path of one's cultural upbringing is well-worn and easy to travel; we rarely examine the cultural influences that have defined our reality since we can remember, or question the validity of those cultural influences in terms of our overall happiness. Truly, how many of us ever stop to contemplate the advantages and disadvantages of high-heeled shoes, neckties or the forty-hour work week?

Cultures can be unequivocal in dictating what their members

must have, do or look like in order to be considered successful or attractive. Those who deviate from social norms are often seen as rebels, hippies, or in extreme cases, social outcasts, so most of us don't risk bucking the trend—even when it serves our best interests.

In the African nation of Mauritania, for example, full-figured women are considered the most beautiful and desirable. Plumpness in this culture is prestigious because it signifies that a woman has access to the financial resources she needs to provide herself and her family with a plentiful food supply. But before you pack your bags and book a one-way ticket to the northwest coast of mother Africa, consider the shadow side of Mauritania's beauty ideals: slender young girls are often force-fed by their families, sometimes until they vomit, after which they are coerced to eat again. The Mauritanian culture, which defines beauty as "big," creates a form of dysfunction that is the antithesis of what we experience in the United States. Either way, our cultures are creating chaos.

Thin and Young are "In"

Of course we are painfully aware that stick-thin and young are all the rage in American culture. Print media, television, and the internet relentlessly bombard us with images of glossy-haired, poreless, skinny twenty year-olds trying to sell us cars, furniture, and bathroom cleansers, as well as endless items of clothing and makeup. Most of us know the images of these women are digitally enhanced and airbrushed to perfection, but that doesn't stop us from perpetually feeling "not good enough" when we look at them. And that's exactly what the shareholders of the beauty industry count on, for how else could intelligent women be coerced into opening up our purses and expending our resources—a whopping $350 billion a year—on the latest anti-aging skin care products, body shapers, depilatory trends, and so on?[11] We're constantly being sold products guaranteed to make us *feel* better because we're going to *look* better.

The "thin is in" mindset is a prime example of what sociologists Peter Berger and Thomas Luckmann refer to as "the social construction of reality." Berger and Luckmann describe our social paradigm as a perceived social reality, a construction based upon social forces and group think. In other words, we the people are creating and institutionalizing our social norms by buying into them, literally and figuratively. Just as the women of Mauritania participate in the creation of their social reality by intentionally gaining weight, American women are cementing questionable principles of our society by embracing the thin-and-young culture. Of course to some extent we're at the mercy of those who have a vested interest in our acceptance of the construction—i.e., the beauty industry—but nevertheless, we willingly participate in the process.

Ellen, a single thirty eight year-old partner in a prestigious San Francisco law firm, shares her culturally influenced perceptions of her body:

When I looked in the mirror, all I could see was a rear end that was too big and mountains of cellulite on my thighs. On the days I'd throw my crow's feet and spider veins into my list of complaints, I'd send myself over the edge. I was so far from looking anything like the women in Glamour Magazine that it truly depressed me. I've spent a small fortune on beauty products, none of which delivered on their promises to help me drop the pounds and lose the years.

Examining Western women's obsessions with their bodies from a historical perspective reveals an interesting swing of the pendulum. In the nineteen-twenties, tiring of chronic breathlessness, bouts of dyspepsia and the occasional prolapsed uterus, liberated flappers ditched their boned corsets in favor of soft silk chemises that gave them a more natural silhouette. A few decades and countless shoulder pads and girdles later, women once again felt confined by restrictive—and capricious—cultural messages; in one moment they must look like Marilyn Monroe, and in the next moment like Twiggy, in order to be desirable. The stage was set for the '70's "beauty conspiracy" backlash that had a certain segment of the female population burning their bras and growing out their underarm hair. These women's libbers, who saw any form of self-decoration as a sell out inadvertently fueled a "pro-glamour" backlash.

Today, the retrogression towards a highly limited ideal of female beauty is more insidious than ever. As crazy as it might sound to the women of Mauritania, being a mere five to ten pounds away from our culture's version of the perfect body can blind many a woman from seeing her own attractiveness. In the Dove corporation's recent "The Truth About Beauty" study, only three percent of the American women interviewed felt comfortable describing themselves as beautiful.[12] No wonder plastic surgeries among women are up by a staggering eighty percent since 1997.[13] And the ideals for physical beauty are becoming increasingly extreme. According to renowned plastic surgeon Dr. V. Leroy Young, the fastest growing trend in cosmetic plastic surgery is labiaplasty - the surgical reshaping of larger or uneven inner vaginal lips.[14] When women are routinely going under the knife to make their labia look "neater," has the pendulum swung too far?

In *The Beauty Myth*, Naomi Wolfe laments, "More women have more money and power and scope and legal recognition than we have ever had before, but in terms of how we feel about ourselves *physically*, we may actually be worse off than our unliberated grandmothers. Recent research consistently shows that inside the majority of the West's controlled, attractive, successful working women, there is a secret "underlife" poisoning our freedom; infused with notions of beauty, it is a dark vein of self-hatred, physical obsessions, terror of aging, and dread of lost control."[15] As our culture perpetuates an increasingly uniform beauty archetype, it seems there is less and less leeway for real people to comfortably inhabit. It's getting downright difficult to stay connected to the truth: beauty comes in an unlimited variety of physical forms. More importantly, real beauty is an outer manifestation of what lives inside a human being.

How many times a day do you find fault with your physical appearance? Two? Ten? Twenty? Two hundred? Start taking a mental tally from this day forward. You'll quickly start to see the correlation between your self-denigrating thoughts and your mood and self-esteem.

> *The simple equation is this:*
> *self-denigrating thoughts =*
> *self-generated misery.*

It's up to us women to challenge our current social construction of reality and to work towards the creation of a wholesome culture of self-acceptance. We can begin the process with ourselves, healing first our own individual preoccupation with physical perfection and youth, and then moving out into the world to weed out the media-driven beauty ideals that hold us back as a gender. Our success in accepting ourselves as we are will serve to strengthen the collective power of women in the world.

Here's Ellen's experience of beginning to shift her attitude towards her body:

It wasn't until I stopped buying the magazines and turned off the television that I could stop comparing myself to supermodels and begin to see myself differently. I had no idea my body image had been so influenced by the media until I took a little space from it. In addition to quarantining myself from the barrage of sales pitches, I began to reframe the way I thought about beauty, especially my own beauty. Every time I caught myself putting my looks down, I counteracted the self-criticism with a thought that acknowledged the depths of my being rather than my surface. I focused on things like my loving intentions, my acts of kindness and my talents. And you know what? I've begun to feel a sense of self-appreciation and pride that's far and away more powerful than having a wrinkle-free face or tight abs.

In the next chapters, we outline three powerful feminine practices that together have the power to radically transform your life and even to reshape our culture: awareness, acceptance and appreciation. The first practice involves being aware of your thoughts: are they healthy and self-affirming or negative and self-defeating? The second practice entails being accepting of all that you are—even the parts of yourself you don't particularly like. The third practice consists of cultivating a consistent appreciation of your life circumstances and the unique gifts you bring to the world. These practices, though simple, are not always easy. But dive in anyway, and practice them diligently, because when they're regularly applied to your life, you're going to be amazed by how much better you feel, both physically and emotionally. Okay, let's get started!

CHAPTER THREE

Practice #1: Awareness
Be Aware of Your Thoughts

Every day, from the moment you wake till the moment you lay your head back down on the pillow, a continuous stream of thoughts runs through your mind. An unbelievable average of sixty thousand thoughts, to be precise.[16] Whether your thoughts take the form of memories and plans for the future, itemizations of things you do or don't like about yourself, observations about other people, or reflections about things you have to do, should have done, or shouldn't have done, during your waking hours your mind is consumed by a constant flow of information.

Now, here's where it gets interesting: of the sixty thousand thoughts you entertain daily, *ninety* percent of them are iterations of the ones you had yesterday—and the day before, and the day before that.[17] Like the characters in the movie

"*Groundhog Day,*" we replay the same scenes and scripts in our heads over and over and over again.

Research shows that just as human beings cultivate habitual patterns of behavior—brushing our teeth for two minutes, having oatmeal for breakfast, driving to work in the middle lane, etc.—we also gravitate toward familiar patterns of thinking. We know that positive behavioral patterns can have a direct impact on one's quality of life, and the same is true of your thought patterns: if they are generally healthy, self-affirming and optimistic, they will enhance your everyday experience.

Our thoughts about ourselves can range from *"I'm so proud of how generous I am,* and *"I love my pretty hair"* to *"My thighs are too big,"* and *"I didn't get nearly enough done today."* If you're like most of us gals, though, the latter statements will resonate and the former ones will read like corny lines from a Disney movie. That's a problem—a much bigger one than most of us realize.

If an acquaintance were to tell you right to your face, "Wow, you've really aged," or "You sounded so stupid when you said that," you'd probably feel shocked, ashamed, and pretty bad about yourself. When an insult comes from an outsider, it typically hits us like a ton of bricks, and we're left feeling wronged, hurt, and shaken by the assault.

Sadly, though, most women wouldn't think twice before making the same brutal assessments of ourselves. And somehow, the feelings of inadequacy that arise when we self-criticize are usually far less intense and obvious than when we're criticized by someone else. But don't be fooled: over time, a negative internal dialogue has an equally damaging impact on our sense of self-worth. The disparaging messages we habitually give ourselves simply result in a *gradual* grinding down of our self-esteem, rather than a single debilitating blow. Because we're not shocked by our self-criticism (although we should be), we don't realize just how destructive the behavior really is.

Your Thoughts Have Power

Chronic negative thought patterns will adversely impact not only your self-esteem and overall happiness, but your physical health as well. This statement is not some new-age platitude with no empirical basis. Scientific research actually demonstrates that our thoughts and feelings impact physical reality. In his book *"The Hidden Messages in Water,"* Dr. Masuru Emoto describes the ability of water to absorb and express human emotions. Using high-speed microphotography, Emoto photographed frozen water crystals that had been "exposed" to various emotions by inscribing words and phrases— *love, soul, truth, peace, hate, I hate you,* and *I want to kill you*—on the containers holding the water samples. Astonishingly, the water that had been exposed to loving and appreciative thoughts crystallized into brilliant, complex, and perfectly symmetrical snowflake patterns, while the water exposed to destructive or negative thoughts formed dull, incomplete, asymmetrical patterns. Your body is comprised of approximately seventy percent water.[18] Can you imagine what might be occurring to the water molecules in your body as you tell yourself, *"I screwed up again,"* or *"I hate my body?"* Alternatively, can you imagine the powerful effect you could have on your well-being—on a *molecular* level—by consistently offering yourself positive, life-affirming thoughts?

In Rhonda Byrne's bestselling book *"The Secret,"* she describes "The Law of Attraction" as the universal principal that our thoughts are responsible for creating our reality. In painstaking detail, she outlines exactly why everything you experience in your life is at least in part a result of your thinking processes. For example: If you are always thinking about how "poor" you are, it's more likely that your life will continue to reflect a lack of abundance. Similarly, if you are focused on the fact that you are carrying extra weight, it is more likely that you will hang on to those extra pounds. Prentice Mulford, one of the earliest writers and founders of the New Thought movement said: "Every thought of yours is a real thing, a force."[19] This early pioneer clearly recognized the power of positive thinking - and modern-day science is adding weight to his argument.

Quantum Physics tells us that everything in our world is made up of sub-atomic particles of vibrating energy. Even your thoughts possess vibrational energy; respectful, honest, inspiring, affirming, rational and loving thoughts emit a high frequency of oscillation (high vibration), and negative, fear-driven or self-critical thoughts vibrate at a lower frequency (low vibration). In his book *Healing with Love*, Dr. Leonard Laskow describes how thoughts and feelings can impact physical health: "Since our thoughts and emotions are patterns of energy and our bodies are intersecting fields of energy, the energy of our thoughts and feelings is quite capable of affecting our well-being either positively or negatively."[20]

The truth is, we're generally too busy *thinking* our thoughts to stop and think about *how* we're thinking (how's that for a mind bender?). In particular, many of us women don't bring awareness to how frequently we think poorly of ourselves. Like any other repetitive action—turning on the ignition or tying the laces to our tennis shoes—negative thinking about ourselves becomes automatic. Indeed, the whisper of self-denigration can become so soft and insinuating that we don't notice it at all. What we *do* notice is an inner malaise, a subtle awareness that we're not feeling as confident, happy and peaceful as we'd like. We want to shake this uncomfortable feeling, but we have yet to recognize that our unhappiness is self-inflicted. We just keep repeating our self-critical thoughts out of habit, stuck in unconscious "thought cycles" that leave us feeling depressed, inadequate and depleted. As Mahatma Gandhi said, "A man is but the product of his thoughts. What he thinks, he becomes." Of course that goes for us ladies, too.

> Becoming aware of the
> nature of the dialogue in your head
> is the foundation of self-awareness.

Your patterns of thinking dictate the quality of your life, so pay really, really, *really* close attention to those sixty thousand thoughts running through your head each day. Think of it this way: if there were a thief in your house, you'd want to catch him in the act before he took anything valuable, right? Similarly, you want to "catch" each negative thought as it tiptoes across your mind, before it robs you of your self-esteem and happiness. Ideally, you will become as familiar with your thought habits as you are with your day-to-day routine.

> *Catching yourself in the act of*
> *a disrespectful thought about yourself*
> *is the key to breaking the*
> *toxic habit of self-denigration.*

Your Feelings Can Alert You to Your Stinkin' Thinkin'

The fastest way to determine when you're thinking negatively about yourself—to "catch" your negative thoughts in the act—is through your *feelings*. If you're feeling stressed, insecure, irritable or depressed at any point throughout your day, chances are good that your thoughts are low vibration ones. Think of your uncomfortable feelings as an early-alert burglar alarm.

It may not be easy to access those challenging feelings. We often have as many defenses against them as we do against our negative thought patterns. Some feelings can be so uncomfortable that as soon as they start to arise, we endeavor to shut them down. You may attempt to relieve the anxiety caused by low vibration thoughts by turning to an addictive behavior—reaching for a bag of chips, a box of cookies or a bottle of chardonnay to numb your feelings. Or perhaps you'll unconsciously divert attention from a negative inner diatribe by heading to the mall, zoning out in front of the television, hyper-cleaning the house or immersing yourself in work. Can you relate?

Caroline, a high-energy brunette who works in the advertising industry, examined the quality of her thoughts in a workshop:

When I started to pay close, regular attention to my thoughts, I could see how I was sabotaging my ability to be happy. If I wasn't harping on my flabby body, I was picking at my tendency to procrastinate or comparing my disorganized home to my sister's—which is straight out of Better Homes and Gardens. The harder I was on myself, the worse I felt and the more I wanted to escape into white chocolate chip and macadamia cookies, strawberry swirl ice cream or yogurt-covered pretzels.

In retrospect, of course, it's easy for me to see how the anxiety generated by my self-abasement was at the root of my compulsive eating tendencies. Now I choose to focus on all the things I like about myself and I'm gentler with myself around the things I used to criticize. I'm grateful to say that because I'm sweeter to myself, I don't feel nearly as great a craving for sweets.

> Addictions are misguided
> and ineffective attempts to
> escape the anxious feelings created
> by our self-critical inner dialogues.

We use our addictions to make ourselves feel good—or at least better than we did. While there is nothing inherently wrong with wanting to feel good, masking uncomfortable feelings with addictive behaviors is like putting nothing but a band-aid on an infected wound. It is simply not a long-term solution.

The Thought-Feeling-Behavior Continuum

Your thoughts give birth to your feelings, which then drive your behaviors. Here's how it usually breaks down:

Think of each feeling as a message from your soul. "Good" feelings accompany affirming, rational, positive, healthy, inspiring thoughts and "bad" feelings usually indicate that you're thinking about yourself or your life circumstances in self-denigrating, irrational, fearful, disempowering ways. Your disagreeable feelings are your greatest teachers—they purposefully draw attention to low vibration *thoughts* by making you *feel* uncomfortable in some way. Like good friends who care enough to communicate something unpleasant for your own good, feelings let you know when your thoughts are out of whack.

If you don't confront your uncomfortable feelings directly and learn how to shift the thoughts that are creating them, you'll always default to the substance or behavior that temporarily masks the feelings, and your self-defeating thoughts will never go away. But if you can develop an awareness of your thoughts, you have the ability to "tame" them, to take them from low vibration to high vibration.

The Untamed Mind – The Unevolved Part of Your Brain

So where exactly do your low vibration thoughts originate? The culprit is your untamed mind, also commonly referred to as the ego, monkey mind, false mind, or the primitive or reptilian brain... And it can be a doozy to deal with!

The untamed mind is the fearful, unforgiving, unevolved, irrational and compulsive part of your mind that, if not apprehended, will loop a disempowering low vibration dialogue in your head—one that more than likely got activated in your childhood. This neurotic and deceptive inner critic will keep you worried about the future, focused on regrets from the past, judging others and feeling like a victim of your life circumstances. It will always offer you some version of the statement *"You're not good enough,"* or *"You're not doing things right."*

Your untamed mind is incredibly influential because its messages seem absolutely real. When you succumb to a low vibration "loop" from your untamed mind, intense surges of negative emotion will diminish your self-esteem and cloud your ability to see yourself and your situation with clarity.

Thankfully, once you know the nature of your untamed mind, you can navigate your way out of your self-inflicted misery and literally master your mind, engaging your affirming, self-appreciative feminine side in such a way that you rebuild your self-confidence. When you do, you will enhance your life dramatically—"re-thinking" your way to higher levels of self-esteem and self-love.

The Tamed Mind –
The Evolved Part of Your Brain

High vibration, self-affirming thoughts—those little gems that can transform the quality of your daily experience—arrive through the intelligent presence of your tamed mind, also known as the true or rational mind. Your tamed mind is like a wise and sensible inner professor whose advice helps you come up with rational options and solutions on a daily basis. It's also the part of your mind that knows with complete certainty that loving thoughts about yourself allow you to live in more peace and happiness. Think of the tamed mind as the more evolved part of your brain, the part that helps you to connect with the "truth" in any situation. When you learn how to ignore, redirect or silence the negative thought patterns of your untamed mind, you'll be better able to hear the rational and self-affirming communications of your tamed mind.

Remember, it is the act of acknowledging your uncomfortable *feelings* that will help you tune into your untamed mind's negative *thoughts*. Just by *noticing* that you're coming down hard on yourself, you disempower the "tapes" of the untamed mind and unleash the high vibration guidance of the tamed mind. Honing this mind management skill, moving from the untamed mind to the tamed mind on a consistent basis, is key to your personal journey into self-love.

Distinguishing between Your Tamed and Untamed Mind

You may be wondering, "But how can I tell the difference between thoughts about myself that are real and accurate (tamed mind) and thoughts that are illusory (untamed mind)?" Once again, it is your *feelings* that will help you make the distinction.

When the accusatory and judgmental voice of the untamed mind comes at you like one of the worst female stereotypes—

an evil stepmother, a demanding prima donna or a bitchy "friend"—you'll instantly *feel* badly about yourself: "*Ugh, I was such a bigmouth at the party last night; everyone must think I'm totally self-absorbed.*" In contrast, the tamed mind, which is definitely gifted with a feminine touch, will point out the truth gently and compassionately, like a supportive and concerned friend who wants the best for you: "*Next time, honey, just take a deep breath and think before you speak. You don't have to fill the space if no one else is talking. It's not really that big a deal that you were a little chatty last night. Your friends love you and appreciate the fact that you have enthusiasm.*" The tamed mind is direct and honest, but never harsh or unkind in its observations. If you pay attention, you can definitely *feel* the difference.

Indulging your untamed mind's attacks is a barrier to your growth. Acknowledging the areas in which you are being called to mature and grow without beating yourself up, on the other hand, actually helps you move beyond those hurdles faster. The kinder approach is *always* the smarter approach when it comes to self-discovery and growth.

The Practice of Building Awareness

Shifting the nature of your thinking about yourself can be a little rough at first; when you've been down the same thought path many times, you've dug a deep groove in your psyche. But not to worry! You can start to fill in that groove simply by developing your awareness of your thought patterns through your feelings. Here are the specific steps to the practice of building awareness:

Step 1: *Stop whatever you're doing, sit down and be with any uncomfortable feeling.*

Create a quiet and still space for your feeling. Sink into it like you would a steaming hot bath, acclimating yourself to the temperature until the intensity cools. If the timing isn't opportune, try to make time as soon as you can to access the feeling while it's still "fresh." Anything you resist persists. Rather than fighting or avoiding any feeling, bring awareness to it, so you can determine what it wants to tell you.

Step 2: *Identify where the feeling resides within your body.*

Tuning into your bodily sensations is a sure-fire tool to help you become more intimate with your feelings. Pay special attention to the areas of your body where you tend to store stress. Are your stomach muscles tense, or are they soft and relaxed? What about your jaw, your shoulders, your lower back—are they clenched? How about your breath—deep and tranquil, shallow and rapid or are you holding it? Relaxed breathing extends all the way into your abdomen, whereas anxious breathing—the type of breathing that occurs when your negative thoughts are producing unpleasant feelings—will be driven up into your chest to create a feeling of tightness or even mild strangulation. Who wouldn't be stressed when they can't breathe?!

Once you've identified the part of your body where the negative feeling dwells, put your hand on it. Take a deep, luxurious breath right into that place.

Step 3: *Name the feeling.*

You can actually hold a "conversation" with that constrained place in your body to access the feelings behind the bodily sensation. Tune into the sensation as you take another full and extended breath.

Say out loud, "I am feeling _____." You may be amazed at how literally your body will sometimes express uncomfortable feelings.

Step 4: *Ask yourself, "What thought is making me feel this way?"*

Many of our thoughts are taking place on a subconscious level so it may take a little effort to bring them to the surface. Do your best to retrace your thoughts in your mind until you pinpoint the *specific* thought(s) responsible for your uncomfortable feeling. In order to access the thought(s), ask yourself, "What was I thinking just *before* this feeling came on?"

Step 5: *Keep breathing!*

Conscious breathing is an essential tool to help you access your tamed mind. Breathe slowly and deeply for at least three breaths. Breathe in through your nose, expanding your belly first and then drawing your breath up towards your chest, and exhale completely through your mouth as you maintain your attention on the area of your body where the uncomfortable feeling is being generated. Making an audible sound as you release your breath can assist in releasing the physical tension produced by a negative thought pattern.

Step 6: *Redirect the thought(s)*

Presently, we will discuss more specifically what to do with your negative thought patterns once you have brought your awareness to them. But for the moment, your job is simply to be as conscious as possible of the nature of your thoughts.

Jane, an educational therapist in her late forties, shared with us how building awareness of her thought patterns through bodily awareness helped her through a difficult life transition:

I was going through one of those awful times when everything seemed to fall apart at the same time. I'd just quit a long-term job, was building a new business and was strapped for cash. When I got the unexpected news that I needed to move out of the house where I'd lived for a decade, I decided to move into my boyfriend's home, even though neither of us was truly ready for that degree of commitment and things weren't exactly peachy keen between us. I was feeling overwhelmed and tense about my life in general and was beating myself up for not being in a stronger financial position at my age.

Then, kazaaam, in the midst of all this instability, I was stricken with a severely "frozen" shoulder. The pain was so intense, I'd wake myself up screaming at night. I could barely move my left arm, which made me depend on other people for something as simple as putting on a coat.

Of course I spent a lot of time feeling sorry for myself and consulting with physical therapists and surgeons, all of whom proposed radically different treatment plans. But what finally helped me turn the situation around was allowing myself to hear the message my body was trying to give me. When I stopped and breathed and went deep within to ask my shoulder what it was trying to tell me, I had a realization. I had been thinking unkindly about myself and negatively about my life and my body was reflecting my inner turmoil. My fearful and self-denigrating thoughts were making me feel "paralyzed" to create change, which was reflected in my frozen shoulder.

The message I received from my shoulder was "slow down and lighten up on yourself." I quit all the grueling physical therapy and allowed my shoulder to rest. Every day, I assured it that I'd gotten the message loud and clear, and now it could relax. I did everything I could to build external stability in my life, which meant moving into my own place and taking out a loan to build my business. As my thoughts became more empowered, my feelings of helplessness subsided and my shoulder healed.

Introduction to the "Witness"

In the Buddhist tradition, the practice of being *aware* of your thoughts is called "witnessing." When you're in witnessing mode, you detach yourself from your circumstances for a moment and objectively observe yourself as you would a character in a movie. This practice of detachment enables you to recognize the habitual, fictional and degrading tapes of the untamed mind and see with greater clarity the *truth* of your situation—the *facts* rather than the *fantasy*. Thich Nhat Hanh, a Zen Master and peace activist nominated by Dr. Martin Luther King for the Nobel Peace Prize, describes it this way: "Awareness is like an elder brother or sister, gentle and attentive, who is there to guide and enlighten. It is there to recognize and identify thoughts and feelings, not to judge them as good or bad, or place them into opposing camps in order to fight with each other."[21]

> *Witnessing your self-defeating thoughts allows you to distance yourself from them in order to see your circumstances rationally and objectively.*

Tools to Tame the Untamed Mind

The untamed mind is an old dog who doesn't want to be taught new tricks, so count on it resisting your efforts to retrain your thought patterns. Keep in mind the fact that self-denigrating thoughts can come from a deeply personal experience that left an indelible impression. A friend recently shared with us that her negative body image came from a remark made to her in fifth grade! She took the insult and ran with it for almost fifty years before beginning to retrain her thinking. With some elbow grease and a can-do attitude, you can tame your untamed mind, too—and hopefully *before* you've suffered half a century of erosion to your self-esteem.

One of the first techniques you'll need to gain mastery over the untamed mind is the ability to speak to yourself in a soft, patient, loving tone. Remember the internal, unconditionally loving mother? No matter how inadequate you're feeling, or how much you've just blundered, speaking to yourself with her feminine voice has the immediate effect of turning down the over-amplified volume of your untamed mind to a faint whisper. When you re-parent yourself—offer yourself the same loving voice *you* wanted from *your* parents when you were younger—you immediately begin to counteract the low vibration thoughts of your untamed mind.

Now, about those thoughts: what to do with them once you've identified them? One approach is to ignore them completely—which is not to be confused with being in denial. The distinction between ignoring and denying lies in the conscious acknowledgement of the thought and the deliberate choice to redirect it rather than indulge it.

The moment you become *aware* of a negative thought that's making you feel uncomfortable, frightened, insecure or tense, put your attention on something else, *anything* else. Focus on your daughter's algebra homework, distract yourself with a good book, go for a walk in Mother Nature or simply say "NO!" to the untamed mind's rude comment, just as you would to an insult from a rude person. Practice saying to yourself, *"Oh, there it is again, that ridiculous inner critic, the voice of my untamed mind. No thanks, not interested in that low vibration thought today; it's self-defeating and makes me feel awful."*

You can also break disempowering thought patterns by replacing them with *affirming* thoughts. When you find yourself indulging in thoughts like, *"I look awful in this outfit,"* or *"I can't believe I said that,"* purposefully shush the strident voice of the untamed mind and supplant its message with a more loving one: *"I'm so grateful for my strong, muscular legs,"* or *"I'm always trying to be a better and kinder person."* The sooner you can do this the better, given that it's *much* harder to pull out of a lengthy downward spiral of self-criticism than it is to halt negative thoughts in their early stages.

The powerful force of gratitude can also shift the direction of your thoughts towards a higher vibration. Thinking of something about yourself for which you're grateful—*"I'm glad my body is healthy,"* rather than, *"I'm so fat"*—is an effective way to counteract the rants of the untamed mind. Gratitude practice is such a powerful mind management tool that Chapter 5 is entirely devoted to this strategy.

Practice taming your untamed mind with little things at first. Having established a solid practice regarding small self-doubts and worries will help you when the tough stuff presents itself. Identify the areas where you are your harshest critic: are you likely to be critical of your body? Your capabilities? Your parenting skills? Your degree of intelligence? Your overall physical attractiveness? Your level of productivity? Is your untamed mind more likely to rear its ugly head late at night or when you first wake up? When you're tired or hungry? You'll be better prepared to catch your untamed mind in the act if you've developed an awareness of your vulnerable areas in advance.

> *You can tame your mind just like you can tame a wild horse, with the soft whisper of your feminine and the strong will of your masculine.*

Untamed mind management is a daily practice because life will *always* offer new growth experiences that activate negative thought patterns. Don't underestimate even a small shift to a more loving and self-affirming inner dialogue. High vibration thoughts add up over time to high levels of self-esteem, and with practice, quieting your untamed mind gets easier and easier. Eventually your mind will get accustomed to the new positive "language" and come to expect it. Be rigorous in your "high vibration thought practice" if you want to feel better every day. This is what is required of us women, given our strong propensity to be hard on ourselves.

How Slowing Down Can Assist You in Cultivating Awareness

A key factor in your ability to recognize and confront the thought patterns of the untamed mind is the pace of your lifestyle. If you're always on the go, chronically engaging your *yang* and neglecting your *yin*, you're giving your untamed mind extra fuel. You're unlikely to even notice, much less attempt to silence, your negative thought patterns when you're splitting your focus, running around frantically checking items off your To-Do list. So the thought patterns "loop" and "loop" again— proliferating like flies feeding on a decaying carcass.

> The busier you are, the more active your untamed mind will be.

It's no small feat to slow down and be alone with your thoughts—really, why would anyone choose to spend an afternoon with a rude and critical person?! The moment you stop *doing*, your untamed mind will start pestering you about all that you need to accomplish (or should have accomplished, or never will accomplish...). This is when it gets tempting to distract yourself with yet another task or treat. But the simple fact of the matter is, it takes a dedication of time and commitment to cultivate awareness.

When your thoughts are running amuck, sitting down and breathing fully and deeply is the smartest thing you can do. This action—or really, inaction—releases your "inner therapist," the loving coach whose job it is to guide you towards something larger than the narrow scope of habitual thoughts and events that define your day-to-day life. Spending time in silence creates receptivity in your very being, so that you can gain access to solutions to problems, bursts of creativity, and flashes of intuition offered by your tamed mind. It is in *being* that you will be most successful in cultivating awareness and accessing the tamed mind.

> If you want to "be" happier, "do" less.

The Bigger Picture

To free up vast amounts of personal power, we must first honor ourselves through our thinking. We must choose thoughts—compassionate thoughts, inspiring thoughts, loving thoughts, grateful thoughts, feminine thoughts—that nurture our souls and honor our beings. The tyranny of the untamed mind can be overthrown when we make a commitment to cherry-picking our grandest and most self-loving thoughts. It can also be redirected by asking yourself powerful questions such as: Is this thought serving me or is it disempowering me?

If you find it difficult to think highly about yourself for your *own* good, do it for the good of those around you, or for the good of the planet. Remember, if you help yourself, you help us all. If you doubt that thinking loving thoughts about yourself can make a difference in your personal sphere, try it for one week solid and see for yourself. Love is the strongest force on earth, and when you focus that powerful energy towards yourself, you not only heal the wounds that have kept you from the joy that's your birthright, but you also transmit healing, high vibration energy to everyone around you. When you ask yourself the larger questions in life (How do I want to show up in the world?) instead of solely the smaller questions, (What do I want for lunch?) you gain access to new and original thoughts outside of the sixty-thousand you regularly indulge out of habit. The larger and deeper questions allow you to expand your life experience rather than stay stagnant in old patterns of thinking and behaving.

So ask yourself, "What's the legacy I want to leave?" Do you want to be remembered as someone that was incredibly kind? Wise? Loving? Compassionate? Courageous? Strong? Knowing that self-loving thoughts bring out these qualities should serve as a strong impetus to choose them if you want to show up in the world at your full potential.

Martin Luther King, Jr. said, "I have decided to stick with love. For I know that love is ultimately the only answer to mankind's problems, and I'm going to talk about it everywhere I go." Can you think of a higher vibration perspective than that?!

*"Compassion starts with making friends with ourselves –
particularly with our poisons."*
-Pema Chodron

CHAPTER FOUR

Practice #2: Acceptance
Be Accepting of Yourself and Others

When was the last time you confessed to feeling jealous of your younger sister? Admitted that gossiping gives you a little thrill? Shared with your intimate partner that you know you can be controlling and self-absorbed? If you're like most of us ladies, chances are good that you don't willingly cop to some of your most unappealing and unattractive characteristics.

The irony is that, even as we carry harsh and inaccurate perceptions about how we look and what we accomplish, we often *deny* those characteristics that *others* accuse us of having—the ones we *really do* embody and that *really do* create problems for us. For example, if our partner calls us controlling when we color-coordinate his sock drawer, we defend ourselves like a castle. If our son says we're nagging after we badger him umpteen times to comb his hair, we accuse him of being disrespectful. And if a friend were to decry us for gossiping as we prattled on about a mutual acquaintance, we'd be highly offended. You get the idea. Owning all of who we are can be tough to swallow.

> *Shadow qualities are the traits we'd rather not admit we possess because we believe they make us unlikable or even unlovable.*

Can you think of specific qualities with which you'd never want to be associated? Imagine standing with a microphone before an audience and announcing: I am...desperate, insensitive, insecure, slutty, weird, stupid, perfectionistic, weak, backstabbing, bossy, lazy, bitter, stingy, phony, egocentric, sloppy, fearful or—a real zinger for us gals—bitchy, and you'll no doubt experience an internal shudder of horror. It's not fun owning our "shadow side"—the side of us Carl Jung called "the person you would rather not be." Nevertheless, each and every one of us has a hint—or in some cases a heavy dose—of every single quality somewhere within our being, including those we find the most shameful, offensive or unacceptable.

By denying the qualities that make us feel "bad," "weird," or "different," we in effect tell ourselves it's not okay for us to possess them. Humans have had a primal need to be accepted by family, peers and community since the days of our earliest ancestors, when rejection by the tribe meant certain death because one simply couldn't survive in the wilderness alone. Our untamed mind still does a good job of convincing us that hiding our shadow from others—and even from ourselves— will protect us from life-threatening rejection by our "tribe."

Of course the shadow is simply part of the human condition, and by recognizing this reality we can relieve some of the pressure we feel to *be* perfect or to *do* it perfectly. As human beings, we're *entitled* to make mistakes, which at times will include operating from our shadow as we grow and learn. Just as there's no need for us to feel embarrassed about bodily functions, we needn't feel ashamed or guilty about our shadow. It may not be not the prettiest part of who we are, but it's a part nonetheless.

The Danger of Denying the Shadow

Denying your shadow can have significant repercussions. If you don't feel safe to reveal your shadow, even to yourself, you won't be able to see yourself with total clarity. And if you don't see yourself with total clarity, you can't ever move beyond the shadow behaviors that aren't serving you. Moreover, when you disown your shadow side, in effect rejecting a part of yourself that's as real as the nose on your face, you activate a psychological reaction that will only exacerbate the shadow quality. Remember: what you resist, persists. By not accepting and owning your shadow, you unwittingly stunt your growth.

Melissa, a stay-at-home mom and school board member, shares her experience of coming face-to-face with one of her shadow qualities:

I heard through the grapevine that another board member at my child's school had called me a gossip. "How dare she!" I thought. "How many times have I heard her telling sordid stories about families in our community?! Dozens! If that's not the pot calling the kettle black, I don't know what is." Thinking about myself as a rumor-monger made me feel horrible. I was so mad at her for making me feel bad that I started talking to other people about the situation, magnifying what I saw as her deficiencies. It was like I was building a case against her.

I was way too busy defending myself to see any validity to her claim. In fact, my unwillingness to see its truth made me default to the very trait I was unwilling to own.

> ## We cannot heal in ourselves what we do not reveal to ourselves.

Your soul has a natural desire to evolve. Often, though, it is not until you get *really* uncomfortable that you're motivated to go within and explore a shadow quality more deeply. If you don't "out" your shadow, you won't be able to determine what that dark quality can teach you. Conversely, when you *confront* and *accept* your shadow side, instead of judging yourself for it, you create an opportunity to examine the fear that's almost always at the root of a shadow behavior. When you've accepted all of who you are, you won't have to pretend to be perfect in an effort to be accepted and respected by others. Your authentic self will be liberated as you embrace your perfectly imperfect humanity and, without guilt or shame, choose to move beyond the shadow behaviors that don't represent the best of who you are.

Melissa:

When I finally was able to admit that I was gossiping, even though I was mortified, the self-disclosure allowed me to break the habit. Not only did I not want others to see me as a busy-body, I didn't want to be that person. After some self-reflection, I realized that gossiping was not only a form of entertainment for me, but also a way to make me feel "better than" other people. I realized I had some work to do around my own self-esteem so I didn't have to bring others down just to make myself feel good.

> When you remove the "mask" and admit to your shadow side, you experience the personal freedom that accompanies total self-acceptance.

Your Shadow Can Be an Asset

The fact is, when you bring the light of your awareness to it, your shadow can work in your favor. Each of the shadow qualities you consider "bad," in the appropriate context, contains a measure of "good" as well. Let's take a look at some shadow qualities that in their extreme can be disempowering, but in balance can be highly beneficial:

- Being a *little* lazy can help you to relax. Being *really* lazy can have you popping bonbons and watching soap operas all day long.

- Feeling angry lets you know when your boundaries are being overstepped. Becoming enraged can cause your Cruella DeVille to emerge and wreak havoc in your relation- ships.

- Experiencing a touch of jealousy allows you to recognize what it is you want in your life. Being highly envious can make you feel bitter and resentful and wreck friendships.

Are you starting to tap into the concept that there's some value in *every* quality that you possess? It's all about the degree to which you indulge it!

Debbie Ford, author of *The Dark Side of the Light Chasers*, asserts that owning your shadow side allows you to exercise greater control over its "volume."[22] In other words, you can manage the intensity level of a shadow quality by "turning it up" when you need it or "turning it down" when it's not serving you. It feels incredibly empowering to have control over the volume dial of your shadow qualities. If you choose the path of self-acceptance and learn to manage your shadow, you'll be able to make it work *for* you rather than against you.

Take Inventory

Before you can gain mastery of the shadow qualities that impact your life, you must become *aware* of them. This requires taking a personal inventory. Acknowledging your shadow requires honesty and courage, and the process can bring up extremely uncomfortable feelings. But the pain will quickly pass, for when you face your darkest qualities head-on with curiosity, compassion, and an understanding that full ownership of your shadow is a requirement for your growth, you begin to experience the healing benefits of seeing and accepting *all* of who you are. Making peace with your shadow side is "big girl" work, the territory of a mature woman. Are you ready?

Let's dig in. Below is a list of shadow qualities. As you peruse it, keep in mind that we *all* have *every quality* to varying degrees. Circle those traits towards which you feel the greatest aversion, ones you know you possess but wouldn't want to disclose to anyone else.

Shadow qualities: Cowardly, ignorant, devious, insecure, depressed, perfectionistic, sloppy, incompetent, lazy, gossipy, opportunistic, jealous, bitchy, hot-tempered, inappropriate, crass, lying, judgmental, boastful, stingy, immature, irresponsible, vindictive, competitive, prudish, angry, compulsive, rigid, abusive, overly emotional, controlling, addicted, cruel, explosive, defensive, nagging, stupid, conceited, manipulative, fake, disloyal, hateful, inappropriate, insensitive, self-destructive, righteous, begrudging, condescending, neglectful, bossy, resentful, snobby, promiscuous, vain, critical, cold, dominating, demanding, conniving, cheating, nosy, inferior, weak, disgusting, nervous, critical, bitter, inflexible, sleazy, overbearing, drab, racist, pushy, greedy, polluting, malicious, odd, shallow, hypocritical, needy, mean, superficial, violent, crazy, foolish, whiney, martyr-like, annoying, power-hungry, narcissistic, fearful, sneaky, spoiled, wimpy, obnoxious, shrewish, arrogant, thoughtless, resistant, destructive, thick-headed.

Next, choose the three qualities with which you would *least* want to be associated. Write them in the spaces below.

I can be _____.

I can be_____.

I can be_____.

Now read each of the statements aloud, repeatedly, until you feel less of a charge around them. The first time you say,

"I can be greedy," you may feel a big rush of uncomfortable emotion, but by the tenth or twentieth time, the intensity will diminish.

A powerful way to befriend your shadow is to look for its inherent gift. It's usually when our shadow qualities are indulged in the extreme that they create problems in our lives, so if you can recognize how your particular shadow qualities might manifest with their volume turned down, you can begin the work of turning those qualities into assets. Let's say one of the qualities you chose was "conceited." The silver lining of this shortcoming may be that on some level you have an understanding of your strengths and you're proud of them. If your shadow quality choice is "messy," perhaps the gift is that you don't allow a compulsion with tidiness to prevent you from being at peace when you haven't had a chance to organize things. Looking at your shadow from all angles allows you to define not only who you *don't* want to be, but also who you *do* want to be.

What Drives the Shadow?

Any shadow quality that's been "turned up" is driven by a fear (something bad might happen), a lack or negative expectation (there won't be enough for me) or low self-esteem (I'm not good enough). Your shadow qualities are mechanisms devised by your untamed mind to get your needs—however irrational they may be—met. So if you're promiscuous, martyr-like or whiney, on some level you're probably looking to garner attention—attention you likely didn't get at a critical juncture during your childhood. You may crave a feeling of control that you lacked in your formative years, and so you become demanding, critical, manipulative or inflexible. Or perhaps you have a deep need to make yourself look "good," so you become boastful, snobby, judgmental or conceited. Regardless of how your own personal collection of shadow qualities shows up, each trait tells a "story" about you and the persona you adopted in order to get along in life.

Here's a brief exercise to help you reflect on your childhood and examine the origins of one of your shadow qualities:

Name one of your shadow qualities:_____
_____.

Reflect on the early experiences that gave birth to, or served to exacerbate, the quality:

_____
_____
_____
_____
_____.

Name the specific fear, insecurity or lack that drives the shadow quality.

_____
_____.

Assess the fear or insecurity—is it rational? Or is it an outdated reaction to an old experience?

_____

_____

_____

Bridget, a successful San Francisco optometrist who grew up in rural Alabama, examines the origins of one of her three "button pusher" shadow qualities—stinginess:

As an adult, even though I bring in a decent salary and have a substantial retirement account, I have a hard time buying anything for myself unless it's an absolute necessity. Even then, it has to be on sale for me to justify it. Sometimes I decline a party invitation if I know I have to bring a gift. When it comes to splitting the check at a restaurant, I don't pay a penny more than my fair share—and honestly I'm thrilled when someone else picks up the tab. I always tell myself I'm just being smart, saving for a rainy day, that you never know what financial disaster could be just around the corner.

I guess I don't have to look too far to see where all this comes from. My childhood was a far cry from luxurious. I always wore hand-me-down clothes and shoes from my older sisters and cousins, and I remember the electricity being turned off on numerous occasions because we couldn't pay the bill. I can still see the stress on my parents' faces as they sat at the kitchen table trying to figure out how they were going to cover everything that month.

I now realize that I've internalized that worry—to the extent that I've become "cheap," a quality I perceive as the ultimate turn off in someone else. The money fears I inherited from my childhood have prevented me from relaxing and enjoying the financial security I've created for myself.

Adjusting the Volume

Once you have a deeper understanding of the events and conditions of your childhood that fostered any shadow qualities, allow yourself to feel empathy towards the part of you that resorted to a shadow behavior in an attempt to assuage a fear or get a need met. If either one of your parents had a well developed feminine side and made it safe for you to make mistakes or admit your shortcomings, you'll be more likely to acknowledge your adult human frailty without feeling like it makes you a "bad" person. If you were made to feel that mistakes were not acceptable, you'll be more likely to resist identifying and accepting your shadow traits.

Regardless of how much resistance you encounter from

your untamed mind, keep at it! And don't forget to keep your sense of humor as you go about the process of accepting your shadow. The ability to laugh at your humanity—*"Wow, I can really be an airhead sometimes!"* versus *"I'm a moron."*—is a *phenomenal* tool for quieting the untamed mind. Offering yourself your most nurturing, sympathetic, and lighthearted feminine voice will act like a balm upon your frightened inner child, and will support your ability to evolve beyond shadow behaviors that are not serving you.

> When you consistently offer
> yourself the feminine,
> you will feel safe to
> own your shadow.

Bridget begins to use the compassionate feminine voice to accept, and move beyond, the shadow quality of stinginess:

My natural tendency is to beat up on myself about having become such a tightwad. But I know I need to be gentle with the part of me that's resorted to being stingy in order to deal with my chronic fear of not having enough.

My new and improved feminine inner dialogue

> is: "I can understand why, after all you went through when you were a little girl, you'd be frightened about not having enough. But you can trust that you'll always be able to provide for yourself what you really need. I want you to enjoy your prosperity and not live in fear of losing it. Being generous with yourself and with others is going to feel a lot better than holding back."

Remember, there's no shame in having *any* trait and the *fastest* way to turn down the volume on a shadow quality is to be honest but gentle and understanding with yourself. As Gandhi declared, "Freedom is not worth having if it does not include the freedom to make mistakes." Wise words indeed.

Your Judgments Toward Others Hurt You

There is yet another side of shadow work that requires our attention if we women want to claim the happiness we deserve—and clear up the crazy notion that we're the weaker sex. This work involves examining our untamed mind's proclivity to pass judgment upon others. That's right, ladies, let's own it: we do it all the time. Whether it's sizing up the colleague we think dresses like she's in high school, the sibling we're convinced is parenting too permissively, or the single friend who always centers the conversation around her love life, most of us are pretty darn quick to judge others for their shadow qualities—even as we deny our own.

What we don't realize as we're pointing our accusatory fingers at others is that there are three fingers pointing back at us. When we take the time to examine our judgments of other people, they can actually teach us a great deal about *ourselves.*

In his book *"Meeting the Shadow,"* Ken Wilbur asserts that our responses to other people's behaviors "inform" us about our own qualities. That is, if you notice someone's shadow trait but aren't emotionally triggered by it, it's probably not a quality that's over-amplified in you. But when someone's shadow behavior *really* bothers you, chances are you're observing a part of yourself you've been unwilling to acknowledge. In fact, that quality that makes your blood boil will keep reappearing in other people until you take your psyche's "hint."[23]

> *Any quality in someone else that annoys or repels you is a quality that is alive and well within you.*

Picture yourself standing in a buffet line behind a woman piling up the shrimp until it's spilling off her plate. Do you feel amused? Self-righteous? Compassionate? Offended? A mild, light-hearted response on your part is probably a clear indication that gluttony is not one of the disowned shadow qualities you need to work on. If, on the other hand, you're affronted, annoyed, or even horrified as you witness the greedy shrimp grubber, you undoubtedly have identified a "little Miss Piggy" somewhere inside of you.

You might be thinking, "Wait a minute, there's no *way* I have *every* quality I dislike in others. What about violent people? I'm most certainly not violent." True, you might never have *acted* upon a violent emotion, but has there never been a moment of extreme anger, hurt or betrayal when you've privately thought, "I'd like to kill him/her?" If you had experienced severe mental and physical abuse as a child, if you believed you were worthless and stupid, couldn't you imagine dragging your life down a path of self-destruction by acting upon violent impulses, rather than suppressing them? In other words, having no control over the dial? Whenever you find yourself resisting a shadow quality that repulses you, you can deepen your understanding of where it might reside within you by asking: Under what unusual or extreme circumstances might this quality show up in me?

Life has a way of making sure we all evolve as individuals and it will *always* present situations that bring you face to face with yourself and your humanity. So when you disown a quality you don't want to accept in yourself, you can count on meeting people who embody that quality to assist you in seeing *all of who you are*—the light and the dark. With that clarity, you can begin to choose who you *want to be*.

Susan, a forty-one-year-old mother and accountant from Connecticut, shares her feelings about a friend's shadow quality:

I adore my friend Laura, but I feel annoyed and confined in her house, which is so tidy and hyper-organized that I'm afraid to touch anything. She actually has her shoes stacked in the boxes they came in, with photographs of each pair carefully taped to the outside. The books on her shelves are organized by color, and her bathroom towels are hung so immaculately that I'll dry my hands on my pants rather than mess one up. The truth is, I think Laura's ridiculously uptight.

Many of us women don't recognize our own inherent value, so our untamed minds attempt to make us feel better by identifying imperfections in other people. Think back to the colleague in the bare midriff top, the sibling with the loose parenting style, or the self-centered single friend. If you're honest with yourself, doesn't it feel kind of *good* to judge them? Come on now, be honest. You can get a satisfying little ego boost when you think you're doing things better than someone else. That's because your untamed mind, which generates the judgments, loves to be indulged and made to feel right. Judging others feels like a mental itch that's getting scratched—and it takes self-discipline to keep your hands away from it.

The next time you notice yourself feeling annoyed, angered, frustrated, or repelled by a person who exhibits a specific shadow quality, remind yourself that this person is presenting a valuable opportunity for *you*. From there, ask yourself three questions:

- What is the specific shadow quality I'm judging?

- What quality do *I* have that mirrors this shadow quality?

- Under what circumstances does this quality show up in me?

Don't let yourself off the hook on this one, sister. The old saying, "It takes one to know one," has stuck around because it contains a large element of truth. Discovering and embracing all parts of yourself is a crucial aspect of the practice of self-love.

Susan:

In retrospect, it should have been apparent to me that I share Laura's obsession with keeping things "perfect." I'm not nearly as hyper-organized as she is, but I'm most definitely a perfectionist when it comes to cleanliness. I can stay up into the wee hours scrubbing my toilets like a madwoman, and I'm hyper-vigilant with my husband and kids about keeping things clean. Especially during tax season, when I feel totally overwhelmed at work, my super-sanitary cleaning standards can go through the roof at home, where at least I can exercise some control.

Since recognizing that Laura and I share a coping mechanism that makes both of us feel more in control, I've been able to consciously turn down the volume on my own perfectionism and my judgments of her. It's ended up being a very positive thing that I've owned this quality, even though my initial response was defensiveness. Laura has been the mirror for me to make peace with, and manage, an aspect of myself that wasn't serving me.

The shadow quality you abhor in someone else may show up in you in a very different way, to a different degree and under different circumstances. Irene, for example, drives a hybrid, recycles religiously, is up-to-date on all the eco-friendly products and donates generously to Greenpeace. It drives her absolutely *crazy* that her next-door-neighbors have a humongous, jacked-up, gas-guzzling SUV. After Irene did her "shadow" work, however, she was able to recognize her own "polluter" side, whose judgments and intolerance were every bit as toxic as her neighbors' carbon dioxide emissions.

So don't be too literal. Just examine with objectivity the aspect of who you are that's trying to get your attention, so you can exercise volume control around it. And remember: we all have *every* quality, whether it manifests itself full-blown or watered-down. We may all be divine beings, but given that we each have an untamed mind, we are *perfectly imperfect* divine beings.

> *Every person is our teacher, and the people that annoy and anger us the most are usually our master teachers.*

Non-Judgment—An Act of Self-Love

When your untamed mind is in control, you'll always revert to judging others to build self-esteem. Put another way, if you find yourself sitting in constant judgment of others, it means you're chronically at the mercy of your untamed mind.

Judgments against others aren't just "junk" thoughts that don't add anything of value to your life. Judgments actually hold a negative vibration. After the initial rush of satisfaction that often accompanies them, they have a tendency to dwell in your body with a weightiness that at best keeps you feeling anxious, bitter or depressed, and at worst can actually create illness. The bigger the gripe, and the more considerable the negativity you direct toward another person, the more you deplete yourself. So it's particularly important to "witness" yourself in the act of judging when you have a strong reaction to someone else.

> *You hurt yourself more than anyone else when you judge another.*

Perhaps you're thinking, "Yeah, but some of my judgments are accurate. I need the freedom to acknowledge when someone's behaving inappropriately, or I'll feel like I'm not being honest with myself." True enough—it's never a good idea to stick your head in the sand and ignore behaviors that impact your life. But there's a big difference between simply *observing* that your new co-worker is self-absorbed and boastful, and getting all worked up and self-righteous over it. Overindulging your judgments is as much of a low vibration choice as spending time with a negative person who constantly finds things to complain about.

> *Harsh assessments of others keep us tethered to dissatisfaction in our day-to-day lives.*

Think of each judgment as a rock you carry around in a sack all day. Some of us have been dragging around full sacks of rocks for weeks, months and years on end. Through the rigorous practices of non-judgment and forgiveness, however, you can release the sack that's been weighing your life down with unnecessary suffering.

Forgiveness—Another Powerful Act of Self-Love

As we all know it can be *really* difficult to change our high volume shadow behaviors. Maintaining an awareness that under the right circumstances you have embodied *every* shadow quality at one time or another, and remembering that your *own* growth is often a slow process, can help you access compassion for *others* who exhibit old shadow patterns. And just as it's true that you harm yourself when you judge another human being, it's equally true that you offer a gift to yourself when you engage your patient and understanding feminine side to forgive someone who's exhibited a shadow quality.

Here's how the forgiveness process works. Let's say your husband has forgotten your anniversary (thoughtless) or you've discovered that your close friend really isn't happy about your good fortune (jealous), or your child has told you a lie (deceptive). The first step is asking yourself whether or not you're in fact ready and willing to forgive the transgressor. You might need some time to soften the intensity of your injured feelings, but don't indulge yourself for a moment more than necessary. Holding onto anger is like holding onto a hot coal—it's *you* that gets burned.

Once you're open to forgiveness, sit down with yourself and articulate aloud exactly what the other person did that created the rift. State the facts in the most straightforward, objective manner possible, keeping any drama out of your tone. Don't pull up the past or speculate about the motives of the offending party—commentary is the biased yapping of the untamed mind. Retelling the story in a neutral manner will allow you to see the event with greater clarity and insight. Alternately, you can write the story down in a journal so you can review the facts in black and white.

Now it's time to address the feelings that have been stirred up as you articulated your story in order to get to the heart of your resentment. Emotions like hurt and fear can often masquerade as anger, so you might find that your resentment towards your overworked husband for forgetting your tenth anniversary is actually dread that he doesn't treasure your marriage anymore. Or perhaps your indignation over your friend not saying much about your beautiful new house is masking hurt that she can't be happy for you after all you've been through together. Maybe you're not just infuriated that your fifteen-year-old daughter attended a party where there was no adult supervision and alcohol was served, but you feel stung that she didn't trust you enough to discuss it with you first.

Once you've defined specifically where your anger and hurt lie, your feminine side can help you summon compassion toward yourself for feeling the way you do, as well as toward the offending party who's working through his or her own emotional issues *which have nothing to do with you*. Here you may want to ask yourself what feeling of fear, lack, or low self-esteem might have activated the perpetrator's shadow side. How might *you* have behaved under similar conditions? Can you imagine being so swamped and tense at work that you couldn't even remember to take a lunch break, much less plan a celebratory event? If you were struggling to make minimum payments on your credit card, would it be hard to feel unequivocally happy for a friend living on easy street? Can you see how a previous blow-up with your teenager might have led her to hide her choices from you so you wouldn't overreact?

You can learn to soften your judgments and arrive at forgiveness of *anyone*, even those who have committed atrocious acts of brutality, by asking yourself questions like: What kind of person would do this? Would it be someone who is highly fearful? Disturbed? Emotionally wounded? Someone who has a chemical imbalance? Someone who is so controlled by his or her untamed mind that they have no sense of reality? When you put yourself in the shoes of the other person, it's hard to continue to feel justified in your anger, or convinced that the offending party needs to somehow pay for having caused you pain.

Sharing your forgiveness process directly with the person who has affronted you can be a very bonding and healing experience that can take your relationship to new heights. However, if your goal is simply to feel compassion and forgiveness for the offender without taking the relationship deeper, you can do so without his or her physical presence. You can hold an internal conversation in which you visualize the person in front of you as you extend forgiveness or you can even role-play with another person whom you trust to play the part of the offender. In either scenario, you give yourself the opportunity of full expression as a bridge to moving beyond resentment.

Even after you've successfully accessed compassion, the untamed mind may try to dredge up the past and goad you back into a judgmental place. If this happens, silence your mental trouble-maker by inquiring: how long do I want to make myself suffer with the burden of my anger, hurt and resentment?

The final step in the forgiveness process is discovering how the experience can serve you. In other words, what is the gift or the soul lesson in the experience that will allow you to grow as a person? Do you need to practice operating from your feminine side? Increase your ability to be patient? Heighten the intimacy in a primary relationship? Love yourself more? Let go of the past? Live more in the present moment? Accept your own shadow? With time and thoughtful consideration, you can ascertain a gift in *every single life experience.*

Since thoughts and feelings can impact physical reality, it should come as no surprise that the consistent practice of forgiveness can actually improve your physical health.

Dr. Frederic Luskin, director of the Stanford Forgiveness Projects, has conducted several studies confirming that the act of forgiveness can lower your heart rate, reduce hypertension and improve sleep patterns, as well as "reduce anger, hurt and depression and lead to greater feelings of optimism, hope, compassion and self-confidence."[24] There's still much for us to discover about the true power of forgiveness—and researchers are avidly pursuing the topic. But one thing we know for sure, right now, without any need for further investigation: forgiving makes everyone feel better and more at peace. Isn't that what really matters?

Bigger Picture

We women are often blind to seeing both the best of ourselves *and* our shadow side. We are as quick to deny our brilliance, beauty, generosity, integrity and patience as we are to disavow our selfishness, pettiness, greed, envy and rigidity. It is just as vital for us to see our magnificence as it is to see our opportunities for growth. When we embrace our extraordinary value as women, and see with clarity the vital role we play in the betterment of the planet, we come from a higher and more loving place in all of our interactions. Instead of feeling insecure, we mature, a verb which means to "bring something to ripeness." At this stage of our personal evolution, unhindered by self-doubt, we can step into our greatness and enjoy every moment of it.

In your journey towards self-love, it is imperative that

you harness the loving influence of the feminine to fully and consciously acknowledge each of the human strengths and weaknesses that reside in you. Owning your strengths actually expands them, much as regularly watering a plant ensures its uninhibited growth. And acknowledging and accepting your shadow qualities affords you the ability to gain control over them, as well as to forgive the shadow qualities exhibited by others.

Through this practice, you will offer an even more powerful model of "woman" to the world.

CHAPTER FIVE

Practice #3: Appreciation

Be Appreciative of Who You Are and What You Have

Given the choice, we all want to live happy lives, to experience daily that feeling of contentment and pleasure that makes life worth living. But in spite of our desire for happiness, it seems to escape most of us a great deal of the time. Why is this the case? The problem, in part, is that we too often listen to the self-denigrating and fearful dialogue of our untamed mind. It's also because we tend to look outside ourselves for the holy grail of happiness. I'll be happy, we think, when I'm ten pounds lighter or when I have a baby, a different relationship, a new job, or more money so I can upgrade my car, wardrobe or house. The irony is that even if we get what we think we want, happiness can *still* elude us. So what's the answer? What's a fundamental key to a life of consistent happiness? Simply stated, it is the art and practice of appreciation.

Research conducted by some of the most esteemed psychologists in the country reveals that appreciation, a.k.a. gratitude, is a dominant characteristic—and quite possibly the *predominant* characteristic—of people who live happy lives. Individuals who appreciate their blessings on a *daily* basis experience consistent psychological boosts that range from an excited little lift to a rush of unbridled joy that mimics the sensation of falling in love. In fact, people who are grateful for what they already have are *twice* as likely to be happy as those who actually have the most.[25] That's doubling your pleasure simply by appreciating the good things in your life—sounds like more than a fair deal, doesn't it? But as we women are painfully aware, being grateful isn't always easy. Especially when you come home from a stressful ten-hour work day to a pile of bills and a monosyllabic husband whose glazed eyes follow the football game as your daughter grouses about having to unload the dishwasher (never mind that you just treated her to an expensive new pair of jeans you could ill afford). "Gratitude?" you may be thinking. "Yeah, you try living my life and *then* tell me how to generate appreciation. I'm dealing with debt, a difficult man and a hormonal teenager."

Your resistance to being grateful when you're in the midst of conflict, frustration and unhappiness is *completely* understandable. Not only can the drama and drudgery of our lives be immensely challenging, but when the untamed mind chimes in with its two cents about the futility of our circumstances, we have a recipe for a mental soap opera of the highest magnitude. *This* is where gratitude comes into play, and ideally a heavy dose of it.

Let's be clear: cultivating appreciation doesn't mean you shouldn't address the circumstances of your life that are causing you hardship. But here's where discernment—knowing yourself and your patterns well—comes into play. Do you share your appreciation for the good things in your life with your friends on a daily basis, or are you more likely to veer your conversations towards the grievances? Are you quickly able to focus your attention on resolutions to your dilemmas, or do you spend more time indulging your untamed mind's "story" of what's happening to you?

If you're like most of us, it's the latter. Whether it's our disobedient children, our cellulite, our insensitive boyfriend, our lack of closet space or our demanding boss, sharing frustrations is a big part of how we women bond with each other. Dealing with the challenges of modern-day life results in most us feeling so overworked and overstressed that a good old-fashioned gripe session can be quite therapeutic. Fair enough, you deserve to express yourself, to release some of that tension and anger. So go for it. Put it out on the table.

But keep in mind the fact that focusing exclusively on your problems without *any* appreciation for your blessings is a big no-no if you want to be happier. Giving your frustrations too much airtime puts you in a victimized state of mind where you're more likely to perpetuate your problems than resolve them. You could squander away hours, days, and even years in that state—so mentally drained by negative thoughts about your life that you paralyze your ability to change it.

> *If you don't appreciate what you already have, you'll never feel like you have enough.*

Conversely, appreciation for the many wonderful things in your life allows you to unmuzzle the genius of the tamed mind, which has some fantastically creative ideas to help you chip away at your debt, negotiate a more balanced work schedule with your curmudgeonly boss, or heighten your ability to create communion and cooperation with your husband or teenager. Appreciation helps you squeeze the most juice out of life so you can drink in the abundance that's your birthright.

A Shift in Perspective

While there's no doubt that life will occasionally bean you with a curve ball that makes you feel like you've got it worse than anyone else, this is seldom the case. You *still* have an *abundance* of things to appreciate and, if you take a moment to think about it, there's *always* someone that has it harder than you. Often much, much harder. When the untamed mind has you in its vise-like grip, a conscious shift in perspective can remind you that the problems you face—although enormously inconvenient, frustrating or painful—likely fall into the category of *imminently manageable*. So how do you move from a "woe is me" mentality to an "I can handle this" perspective?

Try putting yourself in someone else's shoes—preferably a highly uncomfortable pair. There are unlimited alternate realities to choose from, but let's start locally. Do you know anyone who's dealing with a life-threatening or terminal disease? Someone who's lost a child to cancer, or is completely paralyzed as a result of a car accident? Can you imagine dealing with this person's trials, experiencing her pain? Quite a reality check, yes?

Let's take this argument abroad. If you were to trade places for a day with one of thousands of young Nepalese girls sold by their families into domestic servitude or sex slavery, or if you consider the plight of more than a million Afghani widows who are out on the street forced into prostitution, you might think twice about how bad you have it. How about growing up in the Democratic Republic of the Congo, where gang rape has become a chillingly common instrument of war and political intimidation? Or Saudi Arabia, where women live strictly segregated lives under the watchful eyes of male guardians who prevent them from driving or publicly mixing with men on pain of brutal beatings and incarceration—can you see how many of your challenges fall into the category of "champagne" problems?

This is, tragically, only a very partial inventory of the suffering endured by women all over the world. But no doubt it's enough to make even the most aggressive complainer among us put her tail between her legs and swear she'll never again make a peep about the misery of her life. So your car breaks down, the crown falls off your tooth, your flight gets delayed, the hot water heater floods the garage. Overall, things are still looking pretty good, right?

> *By purposefully drawing your attention to the hardships of others, you can temper the heat you feel about your own.*

Rebecca, an entertainment attorney from Los Angeles, had this to say about generating gratitude in the midst of hardship:

I recently saw a documentary about a Sudanese refugee camp, where women were scavenging scraps of food for their emaciated children and then cooking them a few feet from an open sewage trench. Seeing their desperate situation made a deep impression on me. I remind myself of these women, who've been forced from their homes, most likely raped, and separated from their loved ones, when I catch myself throwing a fit because I've been on hold with the telephone company too long, or I'm late for an appointment and am stuck behind someone driving at the speed limit. Or I imagine one of them washing her few items of clothing in that river of sewage and catching me looking frustrated at all the laundry stacked up beside my washing machine. In honor of my sisters across the world, I think about their suffering and pray for them, and this has become one of my most effective gratitude-generating practices.

Brother David Steindl-Rast, a theologian noted for generating interfaith dialogue and examining the interaction between spirituality and science, recounts the following wise perspective on the art of appreciation from an anonymous source:

If you woke up this morning with more health than illness, you are more blessed than the million who will not survive this week.

If you have money in the bank, in your wallet, and spare change in a dish someplace, you are among the top 8% of the world's wealthy.

If you have never experienced the danger of battle, the loneliness of imprisonment, the agony of torture, or the pangs of starvation, you are ahead of 500 million people in the world.

If you can attend a church meeting without fear of harassment, arrest, torture, or death, you are more blessed than three billion people in the world.

If you have food in the refrigerator, clothes on your back, a roof overhead and a place to sleep, you are richer than 75% of the world.

If you hold up your head with a smile on your face and are truly thankful, you are blessed, because the majority can, but most do not.[26]

Bringing your objective attention to how much harder other people have it is *not* the same as letting your untamed mind talk you into feeling guilty because your problems are minuscule in comparison to those of others. Feeling guilty is not going to do you, or anyone else, any good. Rather, this is all about deciding how long you want to make yourself miserable by taking the "broken record approach" to your personal challenges. Standing in someone else's shoes can resuscitate the powerful force of appreciation so that you can see what really *is* working in your life, and then set yourself up to shift the elements of your life that *aren't* working for you.

If cultivating an awareness of other people's hardships can effectively awaken your dormant gratitude, consistently *doing something* about other people's suffering can keep your gratitude *wide awake*. There are limitless opportunities out there to help out: tutor an underprivileged student, sponsor a child in a third world nation, volunteer at your local soup kitchen, the list goes on and on. Guaranteed, putting yourself in a situation where you become intimately involved with other people's suffering on an ongoing basis will do wonders to keep your inner drama queen in check. And, of course, it will help make the world a better place as well.

What Stops Us From Feeling Appreciation

In this century, Americans enjoy modern conveniences that our grandparents could never have dreamed of, technological progress that was unthinkable even a decade ago, medical advances that allow us to live far longer than ever before, and a modern infrastructure that's among the most developed in the world. With these advances you'd think we'd all be kicking back with friends and toasting our good fortune. But, while the quality of life in the United States is much higher than in most other countries, our capacity to enjoy it appears to be unusually low. In spite of all of the incredible advantages we have living here in the United States, studies show that we American women are more dissatisfied and stressed out than ever before.[27] Like children born into a wealthy family, many of us can't see the advantages we have because we've *always* had them. We've simply grown accustomed to our reality which, although not perfect, is filled with privileges and freedoms that our sisters around the world could only dream of.

When a person or circumstance is a stable factor in our lives, we simply stop noticing that "constant." Our cars, clothes, jobs, homes, and even our friends, spouses and families become background wallpaper that doesn't attract our attention or appreciation—until, of course, something threatens one of those constants.

If your house burned down tomorrow, you'd wish with all your heart you could have it back exactly as it was, including that leaky kitchen faucet and the antiquated stove with only two working burners. If anything were to threaten the safety or health of your husband or children, you'd be devastated, treasuring every single annoying tendency and exasperating behavior that used to drive you stark raving mad. Even simply feeling good is something we forget to appreciate, until a migraine, a nasty flu, or a cancer diagnosis makes us nostalgic for the days we enjoyed good health.

> Appreciation is what allows us to savor
> the precious constants in our lives rather
> than naively taking them for granted.

Self-Appreciation

If you want to reap the benefits of practicing appreciation, the best place to start is with yourself. Self-appreciation
is the antidote for what ails you, because it can override the
untamed mind whenever it attempts to drive you back into a
state of dissatisfaction by telling you that you're not enough. In
fact, self-appreciation is the practice that takes the other two
self-love practices, awareness and acceptance, to a whole new
level.

Unfortunately, most of us don't often stop to acknowledge
ourselves for anything. Honestly, when was the last time you
took a moment to say to yourself, "Hey, I'm doing a great job,"
or "Wow, I handled that situation so gracefully," or even "I look
really pretty today"?

As we touched upon in Chapter 2, our lack of self-appreciation is exacerbated by the images we see on television, movies,
the internet, and in print media. The rich, gorgeous, successful,
youthful, uber-happy supermom dwelling in the female psyche
is an illusory conglomerate of cultural messages that has
us running ourselves ragged as we attempt to be dedicated
employees *and* immaculate housekeepers *and* loyal soccer
moms *and* unconditionally loving wives—all while laboring to
keep our bodies thin and our faces taut.

The media and retail industries have a vested interest
in creating a sense of scarcity and dissatisfaction among
consumers; it's their job, and they do it with alarming skill.
They *want* us to believe we'll be happier and more popular

than ever if only we can acquire the goodies they're promoting. So the proud new owners of the coolest car, the latest cell phone, the hottest designer clothing, or the cutting-edge electronic game gadget are always shown smiling, laughing, and surrounded by other attractive people. Apparently, everyone's having a phenomenally fantastic time *solely* because they own the featured product and not because of the others dynamics (e.g. awareness, acceptance and appreciation) that truly make for a happy life.

The reality is, even if you really do have flawless skin, a brand new sports car, the latest designer handbag and a home in a ritzy neighborhood, you won't be any closer to happiness than the average woman if you don't have a strong foundation of self-appreciation, aka self-love. You'll be running a *more, more, more* mantra in your head, so preoccupied by your *inner* deficit you won't be able to fully appreciate your *external* abundance. In *A New Earth, Awakening to Your Life's Purpose,* contemporary spiritual teacher Eckhart Tolle writes: "Paradoxically, what keeps the so-called consumer society going is the fact that trying to find yourself through things doesn't work: The ego satisfaction is short-lived and so you keep looking for more, keep buying, keep consuming."[28]

> *If you don't appreciate
> what you already have, you'll never
> feel like you have enough.*

It's not until you're filled with the internal abundance that accompanies self-appreciation that you can effectively resist the urge to shop your way to satisfaction. So get started appreciating yourself, friend, before your credit cards max out! Treat yourself like an ardent lover and lavish yourself with authentic, heartfelt and consistent appreciation for the qualities you like most about yourself. Maybe it's your kind way with children, or the patience you offer an elderly aunt. Perhaps it's your loyalty to your friends, or the generosity you've shown by bringing meals to a sick neighbor. It could be that your particular form of artistry inspires others, or that you're a great listener. Don't you dare downplay these amazing attributes! Your finest qualities make the world a better place, and giving yourself loving credit where credit is due is like fertilizing a fruit tree so it can continue to bear copious amounts of luscious fruit.

Carmen, a retail clerk from Monterey, California, shares how she started cultivating a practice of self-appreciation:

At first I was a little uncomfortable with the idea of self-appreciation. So I started small, complimenting myself for something, anything, every single day: unloading the dishwasher, exercising when I felt like internet surfing, or being there for my friends on the phone when they needed to work out a problem. Lo and behold, with every passing day it got easier, and I found that my overall mood lifted dramatically through this very simple act. Sure, I felt a little silly acknowledging myself for mundane daily tasks, but the rewards have been so obvious that I continue this practice every day.

If gratitude for what you *have* can *double* your life happiness factor, just imagine what gratitude for who you *are* can do. The possibilities are infinite!

Body Appreciation: Loving Your Physical Temple

We've examined the cultural construction that leads women to distance themselves from their bodies, and how body acceptance takes big-time effort, given our cultural influences. True body *appreciation*, the act of expressing actual gratitude for one's body, is as rare as finding a taxi in New York City on a rainy day.

So how, as you gaze into the mirror, can you countermand the uncomplimentary yammering of the untamed mind, step into body acceptance, and from there ignite a deep appreciation for your physical temple? One approach is to recognize that each and every component of your physical being possesses a design so genius, it makes the most advanced computer look like a baby's toy. Did you know that your nose can discern up to ten thousand different smells? That your eyes are composed of more than two million working parts, can detect more than ten million different colors and, under the right conditions, discern the light of a candle at a distance of fourteen miles? Or, that your nerve impulses, like a fleet of high-performance race cars, travel to and from your brain as fast as one hundred seventy miles per hour?[30] How about the fact that your bones are four times stronger than concrete, that you have 10,000 tastebuds or that your blood travels sixty-thousand miles per day on its journey through your body? Your lungs inhale over two million liters of air daily, the length of your blood vessels could circle the globe two and a half times and twenty-five million cells are being produced in your body each second. With these facts in mind, it's pretty easy to see that the body you're living in is incomprehensibly miraculous.

You may be thinking, "Yeah, but my health is being impacted by my weight and I'm afraid that if I accept and appreciate my body as it is, I won't be motivated to exercise or eat healthfully."

That's hogwash, plain and simple. As a matter of fact, appreciation for your one-of-a kind body puts you in a *much* healthier frame of mind, which in turn inspires healthier habits. Tapping into your body's communications can guide you to your natural weight, take you to the heights of ecstasy and provide you with enough energy to summit Mt. Everest. Not to mention the fact that a woman who loves her body—regardless of the degree to which it conforms to cultural standards of beauty—has a special magic about her. There is *nothing* as attractive as the glow of true self-appreciation.

Appreciation Brings You to Present Moment Awareness

The untamed mind keeps us fixated on the past, regretting or exaggerating what's already occurred—*Oh no! I blew it, I can't believe I did that, my life is ruined!*—or on the future, worrying about what might happen—*Oh my God, the economy's in chaos, what if I lose my job and can't pay my bills?* When you're feeling appreciative, you cut right through your untamed mind's over-dramatized "stories" and access the high-resolution clarity that accompanies being in the present moment. Along with that clarity comes an infusion of peace and contentment, and an understanding that *everything* that occurs in your life represents an opportunity to grow into the strongest, wisest, most loving you.

Many of our difficulties originate when our expectations aren't met, and we can't imagine an outcome as desirable as the one we originally wanted. Losing your job seems like the end of the world, until you pick yourself up by your bootstraps and find a job you're really passionate about. A heated argument with your childhood friend feels like a kick in the stomach, until you find understanding and compassion and deepen your connection with one another. It's a major bummer that all your friends are married and you're going into the holidays without a boyfriend, but in retrospect, you can see how all that free time alone allowed you to pursue your passions as you deepened your relationship with yourself.

What would it be like to have an awareness of the grander

scheme of things *right now in the present moment,* instead of only being able to appreciate life's twists and turns in retrospect? Practicing gratitude can *instantly* help you recognize when your untamed mind is stuck in the future or the past and is preventing you from responding with flexibility and acceptance of what's happening in the here and now. When you hand the reins back over to the tamed mind, you can make conscious decisions to reframe your life experiences—even the most disappointing and difficult ones—with the understanding and grace of your feminine side. *Every* experience, whether it's a rained-out wedding reception, a missed flight, or a foreclosure on your home, has a gift to offer you, if you can stay in the present enough to receive it. Don't reserve your appreciation just for the good stuff, always be on the lookout for the gift!

> *The present moment is where your life is truly unfolding. Appreciation makes it more appealing to be there.*

Gratitude: the Ultimate Creative Force

Your feelings of appreciation are a creative force that not only make you feel great in the moment, but also have the power to draw in more goodies. The "law of attraction" (see Chapter 3) tells us that *like* attracts *like*. So if you start your day by focusing your attention on what you *don't* have, you've set yourself up to feel bad, and in this state of mind you're more likely to perpetuate a reality filled with "lack." Conversely, if you leave the house first thing in the morning feeling grateful for your functioning car or a best friend whom you adore, your joyous feelings are likely to attract even more good things about which you can feel good all day long.

Have you ever been so thrilled about being asked out by a sweet guy, getting a clean bill of health following a medical scare, or landing your dream job, that your happiness spilled out onto everyone around you and your entire day ended up being progressively more wonderful? When you offer a big fat "thank you" to the Universe, it responds with a "you're welcome" that can come in an infinite variety of forms. It's your *feelings* of appreciation that act as a magnet for your desires.

> What you focus on expands—
> so focus your attention on
> the abundance in your life.

Armed with gratitude, there is nothing you cannot move beyond—no problem unsolvable, no challenge too large. Your ability to generate appreciation, even under the most dire of circumstances, is directly correlated to your capacity to solve your personal dilemmas, and to maintain your sanity as you do so.

Daily Appreciation Practice

Morning Practice:

Starting your morning with an established gratitude practice is a powerful way to influence the course of your entire day. Every day, urges the Dalai Lama, "Think as you wake up, today I am fortunate to be alive, I have a precious human life, I am not going to waste it. I am going to use all my energies to develop myself, to expand my heart out to others, to achieve enlightenment for the benefit of all beings. I am going to have kind thoughts towards others, I am not going to get angry or think badly about others. I am going to benefit others as much as I can."

As soon as you get out of bed—or maybe while you're still *in* bed—picture three things for which you're grateful and write them down in a personal journal. Hold the images in your heart and mind to access during the day, especially when you're experiencing frustration, discomfort or any other intense emotion.

Throughout the Day:

In traditional religious and spiritual practice, expressions of gratitude often occur through ritualized behavior. Blessing your food before every meal, engaging in prayer and participating in religious celebrations are all ceremonial ways to express appreciation for the privileges and blessings in your life.

If you really want to get yourself good and high, try bringing an attitude of appreciation and wonder to even the smallest things you encounter during the course of the day: a volunteer blossom in your front yard, a spontaneous hug from a friend's child, or even your dog's excited greeting at the door.

A crucial—and largely underestimated—element of appreciation expansion is regular time spent in Mother Nature. Most of us spend the majority of our days indoors; we drive our cars to work, sit in air-conditioned offices, then come home and pay bills or crash in front of the television or computer. We forget how something as simple as digging in the soil, walking in the woods, tracking the seasonal changes of a tree, going out to the backyard and picking a handful of herbs for dinner, or looking at a sky filled with billions of twinkling stars can fill us with gladness and instantaneously put us in touch with a reality larger than ourselves.

There's plenty of research confirming that interacting with the natural world bestows a profusion of physical and psychological benefits on people of all ages, but don't take our word for it. Get outside every single day, and see for yourself how this single shift in your lifestyle can exponentially increase your gratitude and happiness quotient. The great news is that Mother Nature puts on a different show every single day.

When you're feeling down, open the floodgates of abundance by not only stepping outside, but "double-teaming" your untamed mind. *First*, think of someone who has it much worse than you do, like our sisters in war-torn countries, and second, pick something, *anything* to celebrate about your life: your non-toothache, the fact that you and your loved ones have a roof over your heads, or the fact that you have a sister that makes you laugh.

Sweet reminiscences from your past can also give your gratitude a big fat goose. French philosopher Jean Baptiste Massieu called gratitude "the heart's memory." When you appreciate a joyful experience, no matter how long ago it occurred, you get to re-live the joy of your magic moment as you run a "movie" of it through your mind. Reflecting on hilarious or heartwarming memories can be a really fun ride and this reservoir of joy is *always* available to you *right now*.

End of Day:

Before you drift off to sleep at night, repeat the morning exercise. Finish each day by thinking of three things that occurred during the day for which you're grateful. Nightly gratitude practice will ensure a more peaceful night's sleep and will gift you with additional energy for the next day.

Keep Practicing

Just as you won't see a toned muscle after your very first trip to the gym, it may take a little bit of time before appreciation becomes a habit you can count on to bring you inner peace. With repeated efforts, however, you'll find that untamed mind mastery is the inevitable consequence of gratitude practice. So stick with it, even when you don't think it's working, because it is!

Bigger Picture

It's no coincidence that gratitude is one of the primary tenets of every major religion in the world. Practicing appreciation opens our hearts to powerful surges of joy, the same joy we experience when we feel connected with God, or the Divine, or however you personally define the source of love that created us all.

On a more human scale, appreciation is *vital* to the health of our relationships with other people, and specifically with other women. Regardless of our financial status, our appearance or our position in life, when it comes to accessing the joy that's our natural state of being, we all have equal clout. And if we're truly all equal, aren't we better off playing on the same team?

Self-appreciation, specifically, allows us to rejoice in other women's happiness rather than feel threatened by it. As suffragist Elizabeth Cady Stanton said, "Nature never repeats herself, and the possibilities of one human soul will never be found in another." Acknowledging that you have unique gifts, and that no one can compare to you, creates an inner state of confidence that makes competing with another uniquely gifted woman seem completely ridiculous.

When women are able to relate to one another without the burden of competition, our friends become a different but equally powerful form of family: our chosen family. We are then able to offer each other the nurturing feminine energy that provides a safe haven for the unapologetic expression of our authentic selves—and we are able to model to our daughters, and their daughters, what it means for women to be the best possible version of ourselves. By harnessing the creative power of appreciation on a grand scale, we can unite in a new wave of feminine solidarity and open up the possibility of becoming true leaders sculpting a better reality for our sisters all over the world as well as future generations.

"If ever the world sees a time when women shall come together purely and simply for the benefit of mankind, it will be a power such as the world has never known."

\- Matthew Arnold
British Poet, 1822-1888

CHAPTER 6

The Vision:
The Feminine Movement

As we come to the close of the Manifesta, it is our hope that you've deepened your awareness of your magnificence, your acceptance of both your greatness and your shadow, and your appreciation for yourself and the many gifts you possess. Last but most certainly not least, we hope that you are in heightened communion with your feminine self.

A Feminine Manifesta was written not just to draw attention to the extraordinary power of the feminine, but also to initiate deeper conversations about how we women can contribute to the betterment of our struggling planet on a large scale. Barbara Marx Hubbard, author of *Conscious Evolution: Awakening the Power of Our Social Potential*, has suggested that at this time in the course of humanity, we are about to embark on "the greatest adventure in human history."[31] This is a time in which we will all become co-creators in a new and healthier social architecture where peace is far more prevalent. Indeed, the realities of poverty, starvation, environmental devastation and wars between nations, to say nothing of terrorism and weapons of mass destruction, are urgently calling upon us human beings to collectively let go of old, counterproductive ways of thinking and behaving. It is time for us to mature emotionally and intellectually, as individuals and as societies, in order to embrace more conscious, forward thinking and compassionate approaches to the social, religious and political divisions we face. And there's no time to waste, for it only takes one nuclear bomb to forever change the world as we know it. As Eckhart Tolle puts it, "The time has come for humanity to make the choice, evolve or die."

We women have a special role in co-creating the new social architecture. But before we can fulfill it, we need to bring our compassionate understanding to what is at the root of the vast majority of societal ills.

It is not some external enemy, but rather the enemy *within* that drives human beings to the acts of violence, disrespect, dishonesty, discrimination and hatred that are creating so much grief and despair for so many. We as a species are generally lacking the self-awareness, self-acceptance and self-appreciation that allow us to see ourselves and all life forms as sacred, and to treat each other accordingly. When we lack a deep understanding of our own inherent value, we cannot grasp the value of others and are consequently more likely to engage in low vibration behaviors that, when multiplied, have the power to bring about devastation. Without a deep respect for human life, we are also more likely to turn a blind eye to the plight of those who are suffering. In either case, we are obviously not living up to our human or social potential.

We *can* evolve and turn the tide on the trials faced by humankind. The power and opportunity for global transformation resides within each individual, and when each of us takes on the noble pursuit of healing our own conflicts and developing a healthy, loving and respectful relationship with ourselves, we can lighten our load and free our attention for the task of healing the cultural wounds we've inherited. We can evolve into the *best* people we can be: models for humanity, individuals who are growing us *all* beyond the destructive paradigm that's landed us where we are today. Each and every one of us, if we want to see the world become a better place, must take this pursuit seriously, and not wait for anyone else to make the change before we ourselves do so. We must endeavor to be, as Gandhi said, "the change we want to see in the world."

The terrain ahead is unquestionably steep and rocky. But take heart because every humanitarian challenge we face is fixable. There is no problem that we as individuals, societies or nations cannot solve—and love, in its various forms, is the ultimate solution.

> *Love is irrefutably the most powerful evolutionary force of all.*

Although trusting that "love is the answer" might seem like a blind act of faith or a crazy naive notion, when it comes to our myriad of global challenges, it is in fact the only answer. Do you doubt the truth of this statement? When you stop to think about it, what other than love, could help us solve the personal and collective challenges we face? What, other than love, heals, transforms and creates understanding? What, other than love, mends fences, creates communion and promotes forgiveness? Love opens our hearts and minds and gives us access to enlightened perspectives that move us forward as individuals and as a species. What can possibly compare to this potent force for good?

Love as a means of social or political transformation has been under utilized throughout history simply because it has been underrated by many of us. That's partly because we haven't grasped love's true power, and partly because each of the incarnations of love is sometimes mistakenly perceived as a sign of weakness. Especially by men. In fact, in most cultures, governance from a foundation of loving feminine values such as tolerance, understanding, compassion, cooperation, rather than from a world view emphasizing competition, dominance, aggression and intimidation, would be seen as an alarming admission of impotence.

The culture of patriarchal societies (which is to say, nearly all societies in today's world) perpetuates the myth that men are "stronger" than women by virtue of being more rational and less emotional. This attribute of "strength" allegedly endows leaders with the masculine authority necessary for effective leadership in today's world, without respect or regard for the feminine qualities that make for the greatest leaders. Courage among men is often mistakenly interpreted as a "call to arms," rather than a laying down of them. The desire to be seen as strong and superior, to "rank" high as a nation, breeds a "we're number one" attitude, a childish and divisive mentality that leads to even more conflict and violence.

We see this phenomenon in our own government, when those who hold public office claim we can't be too patient, tolerant or sympathetic toward other countries because their leaders may get the impression we're backing away in fear. The reasoning is that any indication of "wimpiness" might incite our enemies to attack.

Perhaps men's fear of appearing feminine goes back to their days on the playground, when any sign of a perceived weakness would inspire other boys to go on the attack, either verbally or physically. Whatever its origins, the perception that a feminine approach based on cooperation, compromise and collaboration is ineffective or, worse, dangerous, needs to be re-examined. Clearly the masculine approach without the temperance of the feminine has had some catastrophic consequences.

Mind you, this is not a "man bad, woman good" argument. Far from it. Men are victims of existing cultural paradigms as much as women are, and they have their work cut out for them in coming to terms with their aversion to appearing feminine. We women can help men make the transition simply by modeling the strength inherent in feminine ways. When men learn to regard their feminine side with as much respect as their masculine, they too will step into their true power as they move away from the dominator model towards the partnership model. Harriet Rubin, the author of *The Mona Lisa Strategem* elegantly articulates the shift: "One matures into femininity, it is an act of opening one's heart and resisting the urge to dominate."[32]

Taking a more loving approach to governance and letting go of the old masculine leadership paradigm can be scary business. It requires facing uncertainty, and we humans prefer our familiar, tried-and-true (or tried and not-so-true) patterns to the insecurity and doubt that accompanies new ways of operating. And, on a very primal level, we resist the act of making concessions. In *Urgent Message From Mother, Gather the Women, Save the World*, peace activist and esteemed author Jean Shinoda Bolen describes a pivotal moment at the 1999 Peace Conference in Sierra Leone: "When the leaders were failing in their attempts to reach a truce, it was suggested that women should be included in the efforts—to which the male leaders replied contemptuously, "We don't want the women, they would just make compromises."[33] Isn't that the point?

The specific concerns we hear voiced against a more feminine approach to leadership often involve economic security and safety. Fortunately, a more heart-centric way of operating within our society will not require us to sacrifice either.

Riane Eisler, in her book *The Real Wealth of Nations: Creating a Caring Economics*, describes how countries that are consciously evolving toward a more feminine model of governance—investing in caring policies such as universal health care and generous paid parental leave—actually yield a higher gross domestic product *and* a higher standard of living. Scandinavian nations, for instance, "regularly come out high in the United Nations Human Development Reports measures of national quality of life and also score high in the World Economic Forum's Global Competitiveness ratings."[34] Eisler's concept of a caring economics is one that preserves the best elements of current economic models, but takes us beyond them to a way of living that truly meets human needs.[35]

Arguments that governance, based on a more feminine model, compromises national security are equally baseless. Do we feel any safer as citizens of this country since launching the "war on terror," a manifestation of the current masculine model of government? Aggression breeds aggression. Think of it this way: if someone bombed your neighborhood and killed your entire family in the attack, would you go meekly into the night, overwhelmed by your enemy's display of power, or would you be so bitter and angry that you'd want to seek revenge? Chances are, you would want revenge. Trying to conquer aggression with more aggression is like taking a bat to a beehive. Once you strike at it, you unleash another hostile force to be reckoned with. The idea that we can "dominate" other countries into submission is an immature, unrealistic and shortsighted perspective.

Fortunately, in our striving to reshape the masculine paradigm of governance, we have the footsteps of some of the most revered leaders in the history of humankind to follow. Ghandi is a prime example of one man who changed the course of an entire nation by inspiring people to extend love and tolerance. The tireless dedication and sacrifices of Nelson Mandela and Martin Luther King, Jr. to what are essentially feminine values of compassion and understanding allowed the world to bear witness to the massive civil rights advances of the 1960s and the end of Apartheid. For many, Jesus is the most powerful loving role model of all. While many world leaders and public figures are only vaguely remembered for having held high office or having made a stand, the leaders who have ministered to the world as messengers of peace and love are the ones whose legacies are still universally honored.

There are modern-day examples, too, of love-centric leadership that can serve to inspire our efforts. The leaders of the country of Bhutan, for instance, are challenging the old ways of thinking by measuring the success of their country by "gross national happiness" rather than gross national product. This model, because it makes the well-being of its citizens the top priority, has allowed for a population that is reputed to be among the happiest in the world.[36] Although it is not a perfect system, it is nevertheless a strong model for what is possible when leaders truly care about all the members of their society.

For the most part, however, even though some of the most highly regarded leaders in history have devoted their lives to preaching the power of love, it still hasn't been given its due credit. Leadership by love is an advanced perspective that has not yet come into its own—which is rather odd and heart-breaking, when you look at what its opposite has cost humanity in human suffering.

The Next Stage – A Call to Action

So ladies, clearly the opportunity is ripe for us women to show up in the world in our greatest loving power and step into positions of leadership as ambassadors of love and peace. We are not suggesting plugging just *any* women into higher levels of influence. Rather, we advocate for those women who have themselves evolved into diplomatic, wise and courageous leaders; they are the ones who can offer the highest vibration aspects of the feminine to complement the masculine/ patriarchal model that currently reigns supreme. Just as no individual can function in a healthy manner when operating solely from the masculine, the same is true of a society. It's through the union of the masculine and feminine that we can ensure not only our personal fulfillment as residents of this planet, but also the health, happiness, and peacefulness of our societies and nations.

How will we achieve this ambitious goal? First, we women need to shake up our old patterns—our limiting, self-denigrating and fear-based thoughts and behaviors—in order to step up to the plate and lead in the creation of a new world paradigm. In his book *The Tipping Point*, Malcom Gladwell proposes that new ways of thinking may not be entertained by societies until the old paradigm is no longer working. When it becomes obvious that the old model is "cracked", says Gladwell, a new one is more likely to be generated. If our struggling economy, escalating rates of depression, overpopulated prisons, environmental challenges and nuclear threats aren't enough evidence that the model is cracked, what will it take?

Herein lies our golden opportunity to come together as a global family. Some might consider the global family a utopian notion that can never be realized. It's such a stark contrast to our current reality that we have a difficult time even imagining it. But this is clearly not a time for conventional thought, so imagine it we must. Just as we needed a clear vision of putting a man on the moon to make it happen, we have to imagine and anticipate a kinder, gentler world before we can make it a reality. As Dr. Jonas Salk stated in his book *Anatomy of Reality*, "The most meaningful activity in which a human being can be engaged is one that is directly related to human evolution."[37]

The Feminine Movement—Bring on the Ladies

The *Feminine Movement* proposes that the more we value ourselves and treat ourselves accordingly, the faster we will evolve and advance personally and collectively, and the faster we can get to work to evoke positive social change. As we see more women creating peace in their relationships and homes by embodying the qualities of empowered, loving women, we'll also begin to see more women running for office, supporting one another instead of competing with each other, and organizing to right injustices against human beings throughout the world. The inevitable result of the new feminine movement is that the world will reflect, through us women and the men that are brave enough to join us, the loving values that are vital to our survival as a species and that act as a counterbalance to the values that currently threaten us.

> *The powerful force of the feminine is one of the keys to our evolution as human beings.*

There are three powerful and complimentary aspects to this feminine movement, all of which can take place simultaneously. The first requires that we women direct the loving qualities of the feminine towards ourselves in order to build our self-esteem and show up at our very best. The second entails developing stronger, more supportive and less competitive relationships with other women, especially those closest to us. Staying connected to other women helps us stay connected to ourselves and provides a mirror that empowers us to grow ourselves beyond what we knew was possible. The third aspect involves coming together in collective loving power for the benefit of humankind. When women are in solidarity, our power to improve the circumstances of the world will be magnified a thousand-fold.

The women's suffrage movement, which began in the 1820s, is a powerful example of how, when women unite, incredibly positive social improvements can be expected. Our courageous foremothers recognized that women, although different, were equal to men and deserved a voice in the political process. During the century of campaigning it took for women to gain the right to vote, many suffragettes endured social stigmatization, incarceration and even death threats. We owe a debt of gratitude to these brave women who persevered in union with their sisters because they knew the end result would justify their struggle.

A second wave of women's solidarity produced the feminist movement of the late 1960s and early '70s. This women's movement sought equal pay for equal work, and recognition that women are just as productive and intelligent as men. Some might argue that the techniques women's libbers used to bring attention to their plight were anything but feminine, and it's hard to say whether the movement might have been more or less fruitful without bra-burning, male-bashing and angry rallies. But what's indisputable is that this collaborative effort of women enabled us to make significant and lasting advances in social, economic and political arenas.

The suffrage and feminist movements inspired American women to come together as never before. As we engaged in dialogues about our common intention to advance ourselves as a gender and to expand our role in the world, we were exposed to and inspired by each other's wisdom and courage. We saw strengths in other women that reflected strengths within ourselves, and gained heightened respect for one another. These feminine movements profoundly changed the way women perceived each other and themselves.

This, ladies, is the sisterhood we need to re-ignite and unleash on the world. The new feminine movement has the potential to be the largest and most powerful of all, because the intention this time is to make the world a better place for *all* people: human beings of every race, gender, culture and religion. The idea of the collective power of women working in heart-centric union is not just a futuristic concept, but rather a movement that is already underway, led by visionary women who are establishing organizations devoted to the betterment of the planet. Dr. Jean Shinoda Bolen states, "I believe that humanity is at a crossroads and that what women do in the next few decades will determine the fate of life on this beautiful, abundant planet." The Dalai Lama put it even more directly at the 2009 Vancouver Peace Summit: "The world will be saved by the Western woman." There could be no misinterpretation of that powerful message.

Our Role As Women

You, fellow woman, can make more of a difference than you might ever have imagined simply by choosing the wise and mature path of self-love. Do you doubt that you personally have the power to change the course of humanity's history through a simple commitment to increased self-awareness, self-acceptance and self-appreciation? If so, consider the "Butterfly Effect." Edward Lorenz, a physicist and early pioneer of chaos theory, discovered that minute changes in airflow streams could result in grossly divergent weather patterns. In other words, the delicate flap of a butterfly's wings in Brazil can set off a tornado in Texas! If a butterfly can *unknowingly* change the course of events on the other side of the world, think of how much power *you* have to effect change locally and globally when you *consciously* choose love, for yourself and others, as your primary way of being.

> When you bring love to yourself,
> you bring love to the world.

So sisters, the time has come to move forward in our collective power, to bring our wise, compassionate, understanding, patient, collaborative, loving and gentle feminine selves to the table to make this world a more peaceful and joyous place. When we women place individual and collective focus on what we *are,* rather than what we are *not,* we can liberate a powerful healing energy source which up until this point has been virtually untapped. We will unite in self-love and full support of one another to successfully strategize, collaborate and cooperate to resolve the challenges this planet is facing. We'll empower women throughout the world to recognize their inherent value, champion and defend those who are experiencing hardship, inspire future generations of young women and men to step up to the plate and become true leaders, access brilliant answers to the questions that have plagued our societies for generations and shine a light on the injustices that threaten our children's future. The world will see that the feminine is limitlessly powerful, because its very essence is love.

Gandhi said, "A small body of determined spirits fired by an unquenchable faith in their mission can alter the course of history." Just imagine if, rather than a small body, the great majority of us women come together. It will be a force "such as the world has never known." We would be honored if you would join us and the many other women already participating in the next Feminine Movement.

Love yourself, heal the planet.

Peace ~
Lily and Karen

Epilogue

For those of you who feel more committed than ever to making the world a better place, we invite you to join us in signing a Declaration of Intention. This series of commitments - to yourself - will remind you that your connection to something much larger than yourself can inspire you to change behaviors that aren't serving you as an individual or contributing to our well being as a global family. We the authors read them regularly to inspire the best of who we are to emerge on a daily basis.

With the simple act of signing and committing to the declaration, you are joining forces with thousands of other women in the Feminine Movement who are also committed to making our planet a better place. Even if you engage in these practices only a little bit more than you used to, it's a bigger contribution than you realize; we could literally change the world overnight if all of us women were practicing the intentions to a larger degree! You don't have to make a single donation, attend any rallies, take an oath or chair a committee. To be an indispensable part of the movement, you merely have to live by the following declarations to the best of your ability. It's that simple.

Declaration of Intention:

I will honor myself by choosing not to indulge in low-vibration, self-denigrating thoughts.

———◆———

I will accept all of who I am, even my shadow side, knowing that acceptance makes me a more conscious and compassionate person.

———◆———

I will appreciate what I have today, knowing that gratitude can only lead to more abundance.

———◆———

I will not disempower myself by comparing myself to other women.

———◆———

I will withhold judgment against others, knowing that judgments are toxic to me and the world in which I live.

———◆———

I will offer myself the feminine traits of understanding, tolerance, gentleness and compassion, with the understanding that being kind to myself makes me a stronger and more loving woman.

I will slow down in my everyday life, knowing that a more relaxed pace gives me access to the present moment, where my life is constantly unfolding.

———◆———

I will take excellent care of my body, the precious vehicle that is carrying me through life.

———◆———

I will continually recognize that I can create anything in my life that I truly need and that I needn't be envious of anyone else.

———◆———

I will offer my feminine side not only to myself but to everyone with whom I come into contact.

———◆———

I will be an integral part of the new Feminine Movement simply by loving myself.

_____

_____
Date

Endnotes

1   Barash, Susan. *Tripping The Prom Queen – The Truth About Women and Rivalry*, New York: St. Martin's Press, 2006, p.12-13.

2   The White House Project Report: Benchmarking Women's Leadership, November 2009, p.5.

3   The White House Project Report, Benchmarking Women's Leadership, November 2009, p.5.

4   Paxton, Pamela and Hughes, Melanie. *Women, Politics and Power - A Global Perspective*, Thousand Oaks, Pine Forge Press, 2007, p.1

5   Barletta, Martha. *Marketing to Women – How to Understand, Reach and Increase Your Share of the World's Largest Market Segment*, Chicago, Dearborn Trade Publishing, 2003, p. 55-56

6   (http://www.lluminari.com/news_landmark_study.html) collaboration and cooperation

7   Eisler, Riane. *The Real Wealth of Nations, Creating a Caring Economics*, San Francisco, Berrett-Koehler Publishers, Inc., 2007 p.95

8   Barletta, Martha. Marketing to Women – *How to Understand, Reach and Increase Your Share of the World's Largest Market Segment*, Chicago, Dearborn Trade Publishing, 2003, p. 49-50 Women on the Verge of the 21st Century, published in Grey Matter Alert, a white paper from Grey Advertising, Fall 1995.

9   Myers, Dee Dee. *Why Women Should Rule the World*, New York, HarperLuxe, 2008 pg.209

10 Deida, David, *The Way of the Superior Man: A Spiritual Guide for Mastering the Challenges of Women, Work and Sexual Desire*, Colorado, Sounds True, Inc., 2006, p. 1

11 Wolf, Naomi. *The Beauty Myth: How Images of Beauty are Used Against Women*, New York, William Morrow and Company, 1991, p.10

12 Etcaff, Dr. Nancy, Orbach, Dr. Susie, Scott, Dr. Jennifer, D'Agostino, Heidi. *"The Real Truth About Beauty- Findings of the Global Study on Women, Beauty and Well-Being."* – Dove Corporation, 2004 p.11

13   American Society for Aesthetic Plastic Surgery, 2008 ASAPS Statistics p. 3

14   BBC News: New Warning on Perfect Vaginas. November 2009. news.bbc.co.uk/2/hi/8352711.stm

15   Wolfe, Naomi. *The Beauty Myth: How Images of Beauty are Used Against Women*, New York, Doubleday, 1991, p.10

16   Zulli, John. *The Mind Rules: Master the 3 Powerful Principles that Rule Your Performance, Success and Happiness*. San Luis Obispo, Redhorse Press, 2004, p.39.

17   Zulli, *The Mind Rules*, p. 39

18   Gordon, Jon. *The Ten Minute Energy Solution – A Proven Plan to Increase Your Energy, Reduce Your Stress and Improve Your Life*, New York, Perigree Trade, 2006, p. 35

19   Byrne, Rhonda. *The Secret*, Oregon, Beyond Words, 2006, p. 4

20   Laskow Phd, Leonard. *Healing with Love: A Breakthrough Mind/Body Medical Program for Healing Yourself With Love*, Nebraska, Authors Choice Press, 2007 p. 33

21   Nhat Hanh, Thich. *The Sun My Heart*, Berkeley, Parallax Press, 1988 p.13

22   Ford, Debbie. *The Dark Side of the Light Chasers – Reclaiming Your Power, Creativity, Brilliance and Dreams*, New York, Riverhead Trade, 1999, p. xviii

23   Zweig, Connie, Abrams, Jeremiah. *Meeting the Shadow: The Hidden Power of the Dark Side of Human Nature*, New York, Tarcher/Penguin, 1991, p. 274

24   Luskin, Frederic. Stanford Forgiveness Projects. About Dr. Luskin. www.Learning to Forgive.com/about.html

25   Sirgy, Cole, Kosenko and Meadow. February 1995 "A Life Satisfaction Measure" Social Indicators Research. Springer Netherlands, Volume 34, Number 2, p. 237.

26   http://www.kanji.org/kanji/jack/personal/100peop.html - If you know the original source of this quote please tell us so that we can give credit.

27   American Psychological Association, Oct 7 2008. "APA Poll Finds Women Bear Brunt of Nation's Stress during Financial Downturn." apa.org/news/press/releases/2008/10/stress-women.

28   Tolle, Eckhart. *A New Earth: Awakening to your Life's Purpose*, London, Plume: Division of Penguin Books Ltd., 2005, p.36.

29   Gilbert, Avery. *What the Nose Knows*, New York, Crown Publisher, 2008 pg 2.

30   www.xmediapartners.com/How_many_colors_can_the_human_eye_see- qnazoll.html, aboutfacts.net/Else8.html, scienceray.com/biology/human-biology/interesting-stuff-about-your-brain

31   Hubbard, Barbara. *Conscious Evolution: Awakening the Power of Our Social Potential*. Novato, New World, 1998, p.3

32   Rubin, Harriet. *The Mona Lisa Strategem: The Art of Women, Age, and Power*, New York, Warner Books, 2007

33   Bolen, Jean Shinoda. *Urgent Message From Mother: Gather the Women Save the World* – York Beach, Conari Press, 2005 p. 83

34   Eisler, Riane. *The Real Wealth of Nations: Creating a Caring Economics*, San Francisco, Berrett-Koehler Publishers, Inc., 2007, p.60

35   Eisler, Riane. *The Real Wealth of Nations*. p.5

36   Time Magazine.com: www.time.com/time/health/article/0,8599,1016266,00.html

37   Hubbard, Barbara Marx. Conscious *Evolution: Awakening the Power of Our Social Potential*. Novato, New World Books, 1998 p.8

To order additional copies:

Online: www.AFeminineManifesta.com
For postal orders: Goddess to Goddess Presents, PO Box 4886, Carmel, CA 93921

Please copy this page and include it with your payment.

Please send me _____ copy(s) of A Feminine Manifesta:

Name: _____

Address: _____

City: _____

State: _____

Zip: _____

Phone: _____

A Feminine Manifesta : $18.95
Sales Tax : 8.25% in California (add $1.56 per book)
Packing & Shipping: $5.50 ($2.00 each additional)

For book clubs, large orders and international shipping rates visit our web site!

Payment enclosed: Check _____Money Order _____
Credit Card Orders: Please charge my: Visa   MasterCard

Card Number: _____

Name on Card: _____   Exp. Date: _____ /_____

Your phone #: _____

Please let me know when the following products are available:
☐ A Masculine Manifesto
☐ A Feminine Manifesta Audio CD
☐ Yes, please put me on your e-mail list for future events, products and announcements

E-Mail Address: _____

For speaking engagements please contact us through our web site!
www.AFeminineManifesta.com

Please Note: We will not share your information with anyone at any time, anywhere!

NOTES

NOTES

NOTES